CW00660871

Mysticism

Unlocking the Path of the Mystic and Embracing Mystery and Intuition Through Meditation

Your Free Gift (only available for a limited time)

Thanks for getting this book! If you want to learn more about various spirituality topics, then join Mari Silva's community and get a free guided meditation MP3 for awakening your third eye. This guided meditation mp3 is designed to open and strengthen ones third eye so you can experience a higher state of consciousness. Simply visit the link below the image to get started.

https://spiritualityspot.com/meditation

Contents

Introduction

Mysticism is about your awareness of what makes up reality. But what is reality? The ordinary mind thinks of reality in terms of the physical, but the true mystic has gleaned experience that makes this truly stand out: There is more to life than meets the eye.

Often when you hear the word mysticism, you might think that it is the realm of those who have been initiated into some fancy cult. You might assume this is a concept or a way of life that is inaccessible to you, but this is not the case at all, and that is what this book seeks to show you.

There is no right or wrong way to be a mystic. It is not a cookie-cutter approach where everyone must believe the same thing, or else the man in the sky will punish you for stepping out of line. There are as many paths to the divine as there are people. The question is: Are you ready to follow your path?

The fact that you are reading this right now already separates you from the majority of people out there who are willing to settle for the struggle of physical reality. People who are unaware of how much richer their lives could be if they just acknowledge the mystical.

In this book, you will learn about the origins of mysticism, what it means to various cultures and practices, and in the process, discover what it means to you as well. If all goes according to plan, you will be fully convinced of the need to begin practicing when you finish reading. If you already have a plan, you'll find that the following pages will fan the flames within your heart, making you deepen your practice to become a way of life for you. With this book, you have everything you need to experience for yourself what it is like to have an extraordinary life. You'll learn ways to help people who need it the most, using effective methods that even science has not evolved to understand.

The world is amazing, full of magic and wonder. The fact that you are still reading means that on some level, you have always known this. You are now ready to remember everything your soul knew about the reality of reality before it came into this physical plane as you. Allow yourself to explore the ideas within these pages. Practice, and very soon, you will flow with the mystical as though you've always done so since the dawn of time. And, in truth, you have. There is just one question to ask before you begin: Are you ready?

Well then, it is time to learn the truth about you. Keep that third eye wide open for this ride. You do not want to miss a thing . . .

Chapter One: Mysticism – A Brief History

What is Mysticism?

Mysticism is about you merging with the "Divine" to become one. It is also any means through which you gain knowledge of spiritual matters. This means surrendering yourself and contemplating the divine. It's in a state of consciousness that is not easily accessible to most or outside the norm. This isn't to be confused with being high on psychedelics—although some mystical practices do use them to facilitate getting into this state. It's about getting profound, often hidden wisdom, which allows you to transform your life into an ideal one through the spiritual experiences and rituals you perform.

The etymology of "mysticism" has old Greek roots, specifically from the term *muo*, which means "to conceal" or "to close." Mystikos is a derivative of the term that translates to "an initiate." The verb form of the word has various meanings, from "initiate," "induct," and "introduce" to "train," "make one aware of a thing," "familiarize," and "give one their first experience of a thing."

This term shows up in the New Testament, and according to Strong's Concordance, it means to shut your mouth and eyes to experience true mystery. Figuratively, it is about becoming an initiate of the "mystery revelation."

Originally, it was a term that referred to the many dimensions of Christianity in its early days and medieval times. Eventually, it became a more inclusive term that denoted all the various ideas and beliefs around all supernatural or out of the ordinary experiences and perceptions.

Mysticism is not just tied to one religion; it is something you can find across pretty much every religion, whether it's the Indian faiths, or the religions of Abraham, or other religions peculiar to certain tribes or people. This is what makes its very definition a problem. It's a broad and generic term, but you will have a firm grasp on what it is by the end of this book. Let it be enough to know that it's about unity with the "Absolute" and mystical experiences, for now.

History of Mysticism

Now, you will go over mysticism—from ancient times to its early Christian and Jewish forms, on to the medieval era, and then the esoteric movements of the twentieth century.

Ancient Esoteric Philosophies

Buddhism: Followers of Buddhism are called Buddhists. This philosophy is rooted in the Buddha's teachings and practices and originated in India sometime in the middle of the sixth and fourth century BCE. It was a Sramana tradition and made its way through almost all of Asia. Buddhism is made up of two schools of thought: The Mahayana, which is Sanskrit for "The Great Vehicle," and the Theravada, which is Pali for "The School of Elders." Buddhism's point is to sever oneself from material attachments and connections to the ego to overcome all suffering caused by those ties. It's about achieving Nirvana, the release from the cycle of birth and death, or reincarnations known as samsara.

Hinduism: This is an Indian way of life and has the third greatest following, preceding Buddhism. Followers are known as Hindus. It is also called Sanatana Dharma, which is Sanskrit for "The Eternal Way." It's the belief that this religion has its roots in a time beyond time. This religion has its fair share of rituals and practices like Yoga, pilgrimages, rituals, and other eternal duties—like being honest, abstaining from violence, and so on. Its texts are split into the Heard or Sruti and the Remembered or Smrti. Its holy texts are the Ramayana, the Agamas, the Vedas, the Puranas, and the Upanishads.

Tantra: This is Sanskrit for "weave, loom, or warp." It has connections to Buddhism and Hinduism. According to Indian traditions, this religion also refers to all applicable techniques, practices, systems, theories, texts, and methods. There is an emphasis on the importance of mantras. During the common era, particularly in the early centuries, there were Tantras with their foundations on Shakti, Vishnu, and Shiva. Some lineages can be found in present-day Hinduism, like the Kaula, the Kashmir Shaivism, the Sri-Vidya's Shakta, and the Saiva Siddhanta. Within the Buddhist Tantra, there are Vajrayana practices.

Shamanism: This practice requires a shaman who is the middleman between the spiritual and material worlds. The shaman connects to the other world by altering their state of consciousness, using meditation, chanting, special concoctions, music, and dance, among other methods. It is the shaman's job to set the spirit world's energies or beings to achieve a specific goal in the physical, whether it's for healing, protection, revelation, or anything else. Most shamans are called to their roles through signs and dreams. Some shamans inherit their powers, while others are trained for the job by going through initiation rites.

Sikhism: The follower of this path is called a Sikh, which means "seeker," or "disciple," or "learner." In this religion, there is only one God. It came about around the fifteenth century CE, from India's Punjab region. This one follows Buddhism in the number of followers, being the fifth largest religion on the planet. It is founded on Guru Nanak's teachings and philosophies and the ideas of nine other gurus. According to Nanak, one must dedicate themselves to remaining pure, having self-control, and being truthful in all things. He was about creating a unity with God, which means knowing what God's will is and making sure to fulfill that will no matter what. Sikhism is all about remembering God's word and meditating upon it, which is called Simran. Music is one of the ways that followers can feel the presence of the divine. It's also about transforming the inclinations of rage, lust, attachment, greed, and the ego (called the Five Thieves), which keep anyone from spiritual enlightenment. Despite going through periods of intense persecution, Sikhism managed to keep up its evolution and development, and many Hindus and Muslims switched over to being Sikhs. This same persecution led to the Sikhs adopting the order of Khalsa, which is all about allowing others to follow whatever religion they want to and stick with whatever their conscience deems right.

Taoism: This is also called Daoism and is of Chinese origin. Tao, or Dao, means "The Way." It's not the same thing as Confucianism because there is no need for strict rituals, and followers do not need to conform to any social order. This religion's principles are about entering a union with the universe and its spontaneous, unplanned seasons and rhythms. It emphasizes action with no intention, also known as Wu wei, which is about being spontaneous and flowing with the here and now. Taoism is rooted in the School of YingYang's and the I Ching's teachings, encouraging the follower to flow with nature. It began in the fourth century BCE. For hundreds of years, Taoism has held sway over Chinese culture. There has been a tendency to assume that this religion is the same thing as other Chinese ritualistic religions (called Red Taoism or Folk Taoism), but it's not the same thing. Various qigong styles like Feng Shui, Zen or Chan Buddhism, and others have Taoism elements in them. In present-day China, Taoism is one of the official religions that hold sway.

Zoroastrianism: This is also called Mazdayasna and has multiple aspects to it. Practitioners believe that good and evil exist and that it is "man's" ultimate destiny to overcome evil. These teachings are from Zoroaster or Zarathustra. God is known as Ahura Mazda, which means "Wise Lord." Zoroastrians believe that there's a messiah, after death comes judgment, Hell and Heaven are real, and humans have free will. It dates as far back as the second millennium BCE.

Christian Mysticism: In the early days of Christianity, three dimensions mattered:

- The Biblical dimension, which was about the allegory and their secret messages in the Bible;

- The liturgical dimension, which covered the Eucharist's mystery and Christ's presence in the Eucharist; and,

- The contemplative dimension (also called the spiritual dimension), which was about using contemplation and divine experience to know and understand God.

It was the earliest of Church Fathers who connected the experience of "Divinity" with mysticism. With the guidance of Pseudo-Dionysius the Areopagite, who propagated negative or apophatic theology, mysticism came to be about combing through the Bible to find the real meaning of the allegories within and getting to know more about God than just God's names. So, the Bible was viewed as a book with literal meaning, as well as spiritual meaning.

Jewish Mysticism

There are two kinds:

- *Merkabah*

- *Kabbalah*

Merkabah came first and was about the visions of the prophet Ezekiel. Merkabah is from the Hebrew word for "chariot," which makes sense since Ezekiel's visions included a burning chariot with beings from Heaven.

Kabbalah seeks to explain the connection between the Infinite, which has no end, called Ein Sof, and that which has an end, or Ein Sof's creations. This is the building block of mystical thought in Judaism. Practitioners often refer to the esoteric Kabbalah teachings to define the meaning they glean from Rabbinical texts and the Hebrew Bible, as well as the mandatory Jewish practices.

Middle Age Mysticism

The Knights Templar. They are also called the Order of Solomon's Temple, the same one in which they had their beginnings in 1119. There was military order for the Catholic church, based in Jerusalem's Temple Mount. Their primary role was to keep the Christian Pilgrims safe. They had spent nine years working on the excavation of Solomon's Temple. According to the canon, it is esoteric Gnosticism, but more conservative and in line with Christian Mysticism. The Knights Templar reveres the Divine Feminine, and their practices include chanting, energy work, meditation, chakra alchemy, and so on.

The Cathars. Catharism is a word rooted in the Greek katharoi, which means "the pure ones." The Cathars were gnostic in their belief and very popular from the twelfth to the fourteenth centuries in Southern Europe. They were also called "Good Christians" and prosecuted by the Catholic Church for a long time. According to Cathars, there is a good God and a bad one. This is exactly the teaching the Catholic church is staunchly against. It does not help that Cathars believe the New Testament God is the good one, while the Old Testament God, famous for smiting everything, is the bad one, the maker of the physical realm, and Satan himself. It was also their belief that people's spirits are sexless and are angels trapped in the malevolent God's world. They continue to experience reincarnation until they experience salvation and come back to the good God. In 1350, Catharism was eradicated by the Catholic Church and its crusades and the Medieval inquisition.

Kabbalah: Kabbalah means "to receive" or "tradition" or "correspondence." Rich in esoterism, it is a Jewish philosophy on mysticism. The practitioners are called Mequbbal. They follow specific teachings on esoteric matters that cover the spiritual world, the physical world, and the connection between the Creator and these two worlds. The beliefs of this are founded on the Hebrew Bible and other sacred texts.

Sufism: This is also called Tasawwuf. It is Islamic mysticism, which covers the inner dimensions of the religion. It involves rituals, a set of doctrines, and recognized institutions. It was the manifestation of the mystical in Islam. Its practitioners are known as Sufis. Their goal is the "perfection of worship," which they call Ihasn. Most practitioners followed Sunni Islam, but this practice also affected Shia Islam late in the medieval times.

Beguines: Beguine mystics were primarily in Western Europe's Low Countries from the thirteenth to the sixteenth century. They took no vows other than deciding not to get married. They had the freedom to leave when they wanted. Their focus was on being like Christ by taking care of the sick and poor, choosing to be poor, and devoting themselves to religious matters.

Renaissance and Enlightenment Eras of Mysticism

Hermeticism: This is also known as Hermetism and is based on the teachings of Hermes Trismegistus, which bore significance in Western esotericism and held sway not just during the Renaissance era but also during the Reformation. It is based on Prisca Theologia, which says there is only one theology true in all religions, and God gave it to everyone. It postulates that you can control nature, among other things.

Paracelsianism: This is also called Paracelsism and is a unique movement in that it is a medical movement founded on Paracelsus's teachings. As far as alternative medicine goes, it is a very comprehensive system. Followers believe that there must be a balance between humans and nature, for nature is the macrocosm, and human is the microcosm. Before it died off, it had quite a bit of influence on medicine.

Rosicrucianism: This movement began in Europe and is highly esoteric. The foundation is made up of teachings about the spirit world, the physical plane, and all things about nature that are unknown to everyone. There are elements of Kabbalah in this. Believers were all about humans reforming themselves using a secret science to be revealed only when the time is right.

Freemasonry: Made up of organizations of men, this is a movement riddled with many conspiracies. Members of this religion believe that a Supreme Deity is overseeing all life. Women are not allowed to partake in their activities. In this movement, there are various degrees that the adherents must move through. As they progress, they are taught deeper secrets, symbols, and other things. Members are called Masons, or Freemasons.

Twentieth-century Esoteric Movements

Theosophy: This began in America at the end of the nineteenth century and is credited to Helena Blavatsky, a Russian immigrant. Beliefs of this religion are based on her teachings. It is considered a form of Western esotericism, with inspiration from Buddhism, Hinduism, and Neoplatonism. The movement teaches of spiritual "Masters" who are all over the world and have attained spiritual powers and esoteric wisdom. The Masters want to bring back an old religion that the world once practiced a long time ago, a religion that will obliterate all others. Followers of this movement don't think of it as a religion; they believe there is an "Absolute" from which all things are created.

The Hermetic Order of the Golden Dawn: This order is about studying and practicing all things metaphysical and occult. They focus on the paranormal. Followers prized the development of spirit above all else. For enlightenment, they had rituals and traditions. It was founded by William Wynn Westcott, William Robert Woodman, and Samuel Liddell Mathers. They were all Freemasons.

Ordo Templi Orientis (O.T.O): This began at the start of the twentieth century and was strongly influenced by Aleister Crowley, Franz Hartmann, Heinrich Klein, and Carl Kellner. It has four major branches, each of which claims to be the original movement. It was supposed to be just like Freemasonry as practiced in Europe, but Crowley structured things so it would all come to rely on the Thelema alone.

The Fourth Way: This was created by George Gurdjieff and is about developing the self. It is a combination of the three schools of mind, body, and feelings. This philosophy is about people's place in the universe and just how far they can take their self-development. It's about becoming more present.

Spiritualism: This movement is about the continued existence of spirits, even after death. It says that the living and the dead coexist and can communicate with one another. Even after death, the spirits continue to learn, and grow, and become better souls. It is also believed that the spirits are far ahead of humans regarding spiritual enlightenment. Some of these spirits can serve as spirit guides to the living.

Traditionalism: This involves religiously following all traditional rituals and beliefs. Value is placed on knowing the laws of the culture or land in which one finds themselves and following it to the letter.

Past Mystics

Orpheus: He was a Greek philosopher, poet, musician, and prophet. According to legend, he could charm everything using only music. He once tried to get back his wife from the world of the dead and wound up dying thanks to Dionysus's maenads, who got sick of him constantly mourning his wife. He founded the Orphic mysteries.

Pythagoras: He was also a Greek philosopher, credited with the Pythagorean theory. This philosopher influenced the teachings of Aristotle and Plato. He created a school where every attendant had to swear an oath of secrecy. He did his best to avoid all sensual pleasure and favored the idea of an economy in which everyone had an equal stake.

Thoth: He was a deity of Egyptian origin who oversaw writing, science, wisdom, magic, hieroglyphs, judgment, art, and the dead. Sometimes he is referred to as Hermes Trismegistus, or Hermes, "thrice great." This deity maintains the world and settles disputes between gods.

Chapter Two: The Aura, Chakras, and Energy Bodies

What is an Aura?

The aura is a field of energy that surrounds your body. It is made up of various energy bands known as auric fields or layers, surrounding what is known as your subtle body, which connects you to the physical world.

For the Christian, the aura is represented by light coronas. In Kabbalah, it is known as the astral light. Texts and Teachings of Vedic, Native American, Rosicrucian, and Indian Buddhist origin are full of descriptions of the aura. According to Pythagoras, the aura is a body radiating light, or "the luminous body."

Jan Baptist van Helmont is a physician and mystic of Belgian origin who, around the 1800s, spoke of the aura as being a fluid, one that permeates all things in the world as it flows. He wasn't the only one who thought of it as a fluid, as Frank Mesmer even opined that all objects, living and nonliving, had this same fluid, which he considered magnetic and could affect other things regardless of their distance to one another.

The aura was also called "odic force" by Baron Wilhelm von Reichenbach, who thought that in some ways, it was the same as an electromagnetic field and is made up of opposites. The one difference between this and electromagnetic fields is that opposites attract in electromagnetic fields, while in the former like attracts like.

Reichenback figured that the aura correlates to various colors, and more than that, it flows around all objects and has its charge. According to him, the negative pole is the left side of your body, while the right one is positive. This lines up well with Chinese medical philosophy.

Your aura flows and is made up of a combination of colors which represent various frequencies. It is permeable and open to penetration, and more than that, it is magnetic and electromagnetic. Your aura establishes the connection between the physical you and your greater dimensional self. Its color, charge, and movement depend on how you are feeling, physically and emotionally. Some would say that it's the source of health and life itself. When you're healthy, your aura is lively and pulses beautifully in a steady rhythm. When you're not okay, the rhythm changes to reflect that, and anyone who is in tune with their intuition will be able to see that something is off about you.

The aura pulses at different rates for different people. Some have a more intense pulsation, while others have a gentler intensity. The larger your biofield or aura is, the more you can transfer your energy to other things and people around you. If you took a Kirlian photograph of yourself, you would see an accurate picture of your present mental and emotional frame of mind. You will know it's accurate, too, because if you begin to feel differently and take another photo, the change will be reflected. Even in medical science, there is an imaging process that uses your body heat aura to track what is going on with your body. The aura functions as a feedback mechanism to let you know what's going right or wrong within your body.

Your organs all create electrical flow and have their aura as well, but your heart gives off the strongest flow of all. This flow enters into a dance with the nervous system, which creates wonderful whirling designs or patterns.

Some say that the aura is plasma, meaning it is not quite energy, nor is it matter. Barbara Ann Brennan, an auric expert, believes that the bioplasma is essentially the fifth state of matter. Philosopher Rudolf Steiner pointed out that it must be composed of negative mass. Others believe that it is a combination of antimatter and magnetism, which permits the transfer of energy between worlds. This is how Reiki practitioners, distance healers, and energy workers can instantly change the body using their intention, regardless of where the subject is in time or space.

Why You Should Learn to Read Auras

You might hear the aura being referred to as the "Sphere of Sensation" or "the Universe's Magical Mirror." That is because you can use the aura to interpret what is happening in your or another person's life. When you learn how to view auras, you become clairvoyant. Sometimes, what people refer to as "good vibes" or "bad vibes" is their perception of another's aura or the aura of a place. Besides knowing whether you would "vibe" with someone or a place, now look at other reasons why it would be worth learning how to read auras.

You can tell when trouble's brewing before it begins: When you know how to read auras, you can tell when something is about to go wrong, either with the body or in a place. Think of this as an early warning system so that you can immediately do something about the impending doom before things get worse.

You can use auras to get better at being social: Being able to read other people's auras puts you in a position to know how to interact with them. You can see how they feel in the moment so that you can approach them with the right sensitivity and the perfect words for their situation. This way, you're never at risk for being misunderstood or misunderstanding others, which can ruin what would have been a wonderful friendship or relationship.

You can use auras to connect with family better. Since you can tell what is going on with your family on an energetic level, and since energy cannot lie, you will be able to communicate with your family straight from the heart, creating tighter, stronger bonds that everyone will appreciate.

Level up another's self-improvement rate. Many people have no idea what they need to do to become better at the game of life. Sure, there is the obvious stuff, but there are times when it helps to have someone else tell you what you need to hear. When you can tell what people are struggling with, it is easy for you to become that voice of reason that finally gets them going in the right direction.

Auras and Chakras

Sure, the aura can tell you a lot about someone else, but what gives you even more information are their chakras and the colors they are represented by. Some people think that auras and chakras are the same things, but that is far from true. To make it clear what each one is, you will now dive into their differences.

First, the aura is a field of energy. It surrounds all things, and it is much easier to perceive. On the other hand, the chakra is not as easy to feel out since it is an energy field on the inside. For you to see it, you have to concentrate. Your aura is made up of various energy bodies, thoughts, and spiritual energies as well, so it's a lot more complicated than your body.

The chakras are energy centers of the aura. Each one has a specific color, which can vary from one person to the next depending on their experiences and how they express their individuality. That said, the chakras in your body are pretty much the same as the next person's. Everyone has seven of them—barring the minor ones—from root to crown. These chakras are very useful when it comes to healing and clearing blockages. In addition to the body's seven chakras, there are also five other ones called spiritual chakras. These five are outside your body.

The aura might fluctuate rapidly, but your chakras remain more stable. It will give off information about how someone feels in the moment, but the chakra will give even more intel about how they are in their day-to-day life. If you want to create a change in someone's chakra or to yours, there will have to be a change in mindset and habit.

How to See an Aura

While not everyone can see auras, they can learn how to. You are already ahead of the curve if you can sense people's auras or "vibes." It is that feeling of being inexplicably drawn to or repelled by someone. Once you know how to see people's auras, you'll get a better handle on them and yourself as well.

You must understand that everyone has a unique energy field. In other words, you will notice that your aura is different from your sibling's or colleagues. That said, your aura mingles with the auras of everyone else you spend time with. That is how everyone affects one another, even if they're just strangers in the same coffee shop. Now, do not assume this means that your aura needs to be a total match to someone else's before you can both connect. It's just that the more alike your auras are, the better your relationship will be.

Begin with trying to see your aura, literally. You will need a mirror for this. Position yourself in front of it, making sure that the background is white or a neutral color. This is important because you do not want to misinterpret the color you see on account of having a background that is too busy or too vibrant.

Next, pay attention to your forehead. Keep your focus there for a minute, letting your eyes relax and your gaze go soft. As you look, you will start to notice that there is a ring of light, a halo of sorts, that surrounds your head. It begins as white light, not harsh but soft. You want to keep your focus relaxed and in the same area. In time, you'll begin to see a color emerge. The longer you focus, the clearer it gets. Be easy about this. When you're done, you'll probably see an afterimage, which is your aura's negative, like the negatives of a photograph.

You can also sense auras by tuning in to your intuition. You must already be very familiar with your energy at the moment. Now, get comfy, and keep your hands flat, palms down and six inches away from your head. Do a scan, moving your hands down your body, maintaining that same distance. As you do this, feel your energy, and you'll get a sense of what color your aura is.

What Each Color Means

Auras can be any color. An aura's color depends on what matters the most to its owner and their present state of mind. When you know each color's meaning, it should not be too hard to know what others are about.

Blue: People with blue auras are excellent at staying calm in times of trouble or stress. They are survivors who have very calm nerves and are all about balanced living. They're levelheaded, cool, and not fond of doing anything rash—at least, not while their aura is blue.

Green: If someone's aura is green, that means they are a natural healer. They're also amazing at gardening, being a "green thumb." Their energy puts you at ease, in a state of rest. The more vibrant the green is, the more peaceful they are. They're comfortable to be with.

Turquoise: People with this aura are very high-energy. They have a knack for getting other people under their influence, which is easy for them because of how dynamic they are. The stronger the turquoise aura, the more organized they are. They are excellent multitaskers and perform horribly if they're required to pay attention to just one thing at a time. A boss with this aura is the absolute best to work with.

Red: Those who have red auras are very materialistic and care a lot about their body. This color is about the heart, blood flow, and heat. It's a color that has a lot of friction at worst, but at best, it says that they're energetic and passionate. Red can either be highly attractive or highly repulsive.

Purple: This aura is about the spiritual. If you have this color, your thoughts are mostly spiritually inclined. It's like a cloud or flame. This color indicates spiritual sensitivity, wisdom, and psychic abilities.

Yellow: People with yellow auras are intelligent and full of inspiration. They are often awakening in their spiritual journey. Their hearts are full of joy, and they're the most generous souls you will ever meet. Having a yellow halo means that they're highly developed in spirit and that they're the best person to turn to when you want spiritual growth.

Pink: This is a blend of red and purple, which are the lowest and highest frequencies of colors, respectively. This aura is a rare one. It pops up ever so briefly, inspired by a fleeting thought. It shows that you have found a way to connect your spiritual and material lives seamlessly.

Gray and Brown: These colors are murky and mean nothing but negativity. You will notice them as being much darker than the background as you see them, and they appear to be like smoke or a dark glow. They could mean anything from dark and dangerous thoughts, anger, and depression, to sickness and death.

White: This aura means that there is no balance or connection between the body and the mind. It tends to be a lot stronger just before one passes on.

The Chakra System

The chakras in your body are spinning vortexes of pure energy, caused by the connection between your physical body and consciousness. They act as the hotspots for receiving, assimilating, and transmitting vital life force. Thanks to your chakras, you can experience growth and go about your day.

The word chakra is etymologically derived from the Sanskrit word, which means "disk" or "wheel." It sprung up from India's ancient Yoga systems, particularly from Tantra. Your chakras are in a straight line along your spine. They start at the base of your spine and run up to the top of your head. They are correlated with respiration, procreation, and digestive processes and are connected to your endocrine glands and major nerve ganglia in your body. It would be pertinent to point out that while your chakras are in your body, you cannot see them because they are not physical. Don't expect that your surgeon could operate on them, but just because they aren't physical doesn't mean they don't affect you in one way or another.

Psychologically, your chakras are linked to your emotions, mind, and spirit, especially in the areas of comprehension, awareness, love, power, communication, sex, and survival. Think of them as programs running within you that let you know what you need to do to survive and thrive. For instance, your base or first chakra lets you know when you should grab a bite to eat and when you should work out. Your sacral chakra lets you know what you like in terms of sex and what lines you will and won't cross. When you do work on any chakra, the idea is to look at the programs you're running, get rid of what doesn't serve you, and replace it with something better.

Again, you have other chakras besides the major ones. You will find several of them in your feet and hands, for instance. If you work with your hands a lot, you likely have very active hand chakras. If you move around a lot, or you're an athlete or a runner, your feet chakras might be very active.

Here are the major chakras that you need to know about:

- **The Muladhara:** The first chakra at the base of the spine. To be precise, it is at your perineum. It is also called the root chakra and is connected to the Earth element. Psychologically, it's about being grounded and surviving life. The emotion connected with this chakra is that of stillness. The glands that correlate with the Muladhara are the adrenals. It's also connected to your large intestine, bones, and legs. When it's out of balance, the result is hemorrhoids, obesity, and constipation.

- **The Swadhisthana:** The sacral chakra is located in your lower abdomen. It represents the water element and is responsible for your sexuality and emotions. It drives your desires and inspires your tears. This chakra is connected to your testicles, prostate, ovaries, genitals, bladder, kidneys, and womb. An out-of-balance Swadhisthana leads to frigidity, impotence, bladder, and uterine issues.

- **The Manipura:** This third chakra is found in the solar plexus. It represents fire. Psychologically, it is responsible for your will and power. It allows you to feel joy, anger, and laughter. It matches your pancreas and is also associated with your musculature and stomach. When it's out of balance, you get diabetes, ulcers, and hypoglycemia.

- **The Anahata:** The heart chakra, which represents air. It allows you to love and have balance in your life. Not only that, but it is also the chakra that makes it possible for you to be compassionate. It stands in for your thymus and other body parts like your hands, arms, heart, and lungs. If you suffer from high blood pressure or asthma, your Anahata probably needs to be balanced.

• **The Vishuddha:** The throat chakra, which covers all things related to the ether and sound. It is the chakra that allows you to be creative and express or communicate your ideas. The emotions it causes you to feel are excitement and expansion. It's connected to your thyroid and hypothalamus, ears, arms, throat, mouth, and hands. When it's out of balance, you get thyroid problems, the flu, and colds.

• **The Ajna:** The third eye chakra, which is in between your eyebrows and just slightly above them. It represents the element of light. It is the reason you can imagine, and when stimulated, it gives you clairvoyance. The Ajna is responsible for dreams, which makes sense, as it's connected to your pineal gland. It's also connected to your eyes. When your Ajna is out of balance, you suffer from nightmares, headaches, and blindness.

• **The Sahasrara:** This is the crown chakra, which is right at the top of your head. It represents thought. It gives you the ability to understand and know. It inspires the emotion of bliss within you. Connected to your pituitary and pineal glands, the Sahasrara is what connects you to the spiritual. It is also closely connected to your cerebral cortex and central nervous system. When it's out of whack, you deal with feeling alienated, depressed, and confused.

Chapter Three: Practical Energy Work

How to Sense Energy

Sensing energy is an ability that will take you time to get good at. While you can see with your eyes and hear with your ears, there is no specialized organ for sensing energy. So, how exactly do you make it work? You need to keep an open, focused mind to detect energy.

Everything is energy. You have energy around and within you. The trouble is, it is much easier for you to notice the energy within your body since it is your body, but with practice, you can extend your sensing abilities beyond yourself.

That said, it would be best to begin with you. Besides using your hands to feel yourself, you can use your inner awareness to feel what is going on with you. It simply requires you to direct your awareness to whatever part of your body you choose. You should start with your hands since this part of the body is very sensitive to energy.

1. Stand or sit as comfortably as you can, keeping a straight back.

2. Hold out your palms, keeping them at chest level and two inches apart. You want your palms to face each other.

3. Pay attention to your hands, channel your awareness or attention to your palms, and notice the distance between them.

4. Breathe in, and as you do, pull your palms gently away from each other.

5. Breathe out as you bring them back together again.

6. Keep up the breathing and hand movements, keeping your mind relaxed as you focus gently on your palms and the changing space between them. You may feel a magnetic push and pull cold, heat, pressure, electricity, tingling, or lightness. These sensations are all your growing awareness of energy.

7. When minutes have passed, drop your hands, and then inhale and exhale thrice, deeply each time.

How to Create an Energy Ball

If you have ever needed a shot of energy without the caffeine jitters you get from your favorite coffee, you will want to learn how to create an energy ball. Even more than energy, it is great because you can use it to become a better manifesto. An energy ball is made up of energy, which is the life force or prana, or chi if you prefer.

You can use an energy ball to give you strength when you are feeling burned out. If you're feeling a little ill, you can use an energy ball to make it suck less. If your pet is out of sorts, you can heal them with the energy ball. Want protection? Create an energy ball and surround yourself with it. Energy balls can also bring you closer to divine beings. Best of all, they are amazing for speeding up your manifestations.

Energy balls are actual balls of energy that you create between your hands. You've already had an experience of this from the earlier exercise. You can generate this energy because there are chakras on each palm. When your palm chakras are open and balanced, you're at ease with getting compliments because you have a high sense of self-worth. You praise yourself for your amazing skills and talents and do not talk yourself down. If you're a writer, the words flow. You're cool with hearing others out, even if they see things differently than you do. You know when you walk into a room whether you should be there or not. You have a sense of things and just know when something is good or not.

Here is how to create an energy ball:

1. Find a quiet place where you won't be disturbed and get rid of all distractions. Ask not to be interrupted.

2. Sit in a comfy position, and focus on your breath for a few minutes, until you feel at peace.

3. Imagine the energy in the form of light, coming down from the crown of your head and going right into the ground just like tree roots. Imagine the earth sending up its energy through you.

4. Put your palms at chest level, facing each other, with just a few inches apart. You can also put one palm over the other, if you prefer, keeping the distance between them.

5. Breathe in and out deeply as you move your hands gently in a circle.

6. In your mind's eye, visualize a ball of white light starting to form in the middle of your palms. Feel its heat and magnetism.

7. As you move your hands, you will start to notice that they move further and further apart. This is because the ball is getting bigger.

8. You can now program the ball with your intentions. If you want to heal yourself with it, imagine it connecting with your solar plexus chakra and feel the energy going back and forth between the ball and this chakra.

9. If there's a spot on your body that hurts, move the ball there with the intention to heal it.

10. You can move the ball around your pet if they need healing or to be calmed.

11. You can also visualize something you want to happen and then release the ball to go out and do your bidding.

How to Sense Chakras

1. Before you begin, make sure you refer to the section on chakras to know exactly where they should be.

2. Now, you'll need a partner for this. Let them lie on a bed or a massage table if you've got one.

3. Keep your hands above their body, just a few inches apart.

4. Slowly move your hands along the middle of their body, beginning just beneath the groin, making your way up to the top of their head. As you move your hands, see if you sense any difference in energy where the chakras should be. You might see colors or pictures that tie into the chakra, but it's more likely that you just feel the energy with your hands.

Note: The ability to sense chakras differs from one person to another. Some people feel warmth; others feel coolness. Some people get a buzz in their hands. Either way, the more you practice, the better you will get at sensing the chakras. If you find that you do not have the words to describe what you feel, that is fine. The point is that you can sense or feel something at each chakra.

Some chakras will give you more information than others, and you might feel when there is an imbalance or when there's a release. It all depends on who you are dealing with and what they're dealing with in their life. If you don't sense anything, do not allow yourself to be discouraged. It is okay to imagine that you do sense the chakras. Imagination will allow you to unlock your psychic abilities. Finally, do not allow yourself to be doubtful. Here is a good rule of thumb: If you think you can sense something as you practice, you sensed it. The more you trust your abilities, the better you will get.

Sensing Chakras Using a Pendulum

A pendulum is a little, weighty object that hangs from a short chain or string. Ideally, it should be something meaningful to you, something that you can visually appreciate, whether it is a crystal, stylized key, stone, or whatever else that matters. Here's how to use it to sense chakras:

1. Hold your pendulum above your chakra. Make sure it hangs above this chakra by a few inches. Wait until it gets completely still.

2. After a short period, your pendulum will begin moving.

3. When it moves clockwise, it means things are okay with the chakra.

4. When it moves counterclockwise, the chakra's spinning, but in the opposite direction.

5. When the pendulum is completely still or moves only in small circles, that chakra isn't very active.

6. When the chakra moves in large circles, it is way too active.

7. When it moves in a moderate circle and clockwise, the chakra is just fine.

Opening Your Chakras

Whenever you are feeling a bit off, stressed out, or just down, it could be that your chakras are blocked, and therefore, the energy does not flow freely in your body and mind. Here is how to open your chakras:

1. *Practice Meditation:* When you meditate, you get in touch with the dimensionally larger aspect of your being, which allows you to connect to the boundless energy around you. This practice allows you to eliminate the troublesome thoughts and emotions that block your energy from the free flow. As you meditate, you allow clean, new energy to begin to circulate within and around you as your chakras open, thanks to this practice.

To meditate, simply pick a time of day and ask not to be disturbed. Wear loose, comfortable clothing. Sit up in a comfy chair, shut your eyes, part your lips slightly, and pay attention to your breathing. Breathe in, filling your belly and lungs with air. Hold that breath for a couple of seconds and then release it slowly through your slightly parted lips. When thoughts distract you, know it's not a big deal. Be glad you noticed and return your attention to your breathing. Never beat yourself up for getting distracted. The fact that you notice each time your mind wanders is progress.

2. *Practice Yoga:* Yoga is great for getting the energy in your body moving again. Each pose does wonders for each chakra. For your root chakra, do child's pose, warrior 1, tree pose, and eagle pose. The sacral chakra or svadhisthana benefits from pigeon pose, goddess pose, and dancer's pose. For your solar plexus, try out the boat pose and mountain pose. Sun salutations also get the energy moving in that chakra. For your anahata, you should do the up-dog, camel, and cobra poses. Your throat chakra will open when you make the shoulder stand and headstand—both supported—and when you circle

your neck. For your third eye, you want to practice the cat and cow pose and the easy and child's poses. Finally, for your crown chakra, do the corpse pose (also called savasana) and the headstand.

3. *Use Affirmations and Mantras*: Mantras are words that have power in them. They're mystical in origin and have various effects. Affirmations are also wonderful to help you open your chakras for more energy flow. You can use both as you meditate, or you can simply use them all through your day by saying them in your mind or out loud. To open your root chakra, chant the mantra "Lam" over and over as you meditate. For your sacral chakra, "Ram" is the mantra to chant. Chant "Yam" to open and balance your heart chakra. "Ham" will unblock your throat chakra, while "Aum" (or "Om") will clear out your third eye. Finally, for the sahasrara, you don't chant. You just listen. Listen to the moment, to all sounds you hear. Don't try to pick them out. Just be still and be aware of how each sound makes up one sound.

4. *Use Creative Visualization*: This is a great way to clear out all energetic blocks within you. Get relaxed, either on your favorite chair or a comfy bed. If you can, get out in nature and just lie on the grass, soaking up that good energy all around you. Next, shut your eyes and begin to think of colors and snapshots that remind you of happiness, goodness, and love. As you lay there, you can also imagine yourself being in a place that makes you incredibly happy. Next, imagine a flower that matches each of your chakras. See their petals opening and becoming more vibrant, deeper in color and beauty. Do this for each chakra.

5. *Conscious Breathing*: Most of us breathe on autopilot, without having to think about it. This is by design, and it's a good thing you don't have to worry about it; otherwise, in today's distraction laden culture, you would forget to breathe.

To open and balance your chakras, you should learn to breathe consciously.

First, sit somewhere quiet and relax. No distractions. Now, you're going to breathe in, and as you do, direct your awareness to your root chakra. Imagine a divine, white light going into your root chakra as you inhale, charging it, waking it up. As you exhale, imagine that your chakra expels dark energy and feels freer. Do this until the root chakra is a clear, vibrant red in your visualization. Now repeat this process with the sacral chakra, moving through all the others until you reach the crown.

6. *Be Forgiving.* If there's someone you're holding a grudge against, you need to forgive them. If you're drowning in regret, angry at yourself or someone else, grieving over the loss of a loved one or something special, you will need to learn to let it all go. Forgive yourself, and forgive others, so you can set yourself free. Otherwise, holding on to these murky emotions will block your chakras. If you think, "Blocked chakras, so what? Big whoop, life sucks," well, these blockages can begin to affect you physically, and you could get nasty diseases and illnesses, which you definitely could do without. So, let go. Do what you must to let go. You could do a ritual, cry, move your body, meditate, spend more time with mother nature, or get a pet and learn to channel love to it. You could also get help from a professional who can help you see your way through moving on for the better.

7. *Practice Gratitude.* This is a little too underrated. Gratitude is amazing because there's no better, faster way to banish bad vibes, boost your energy, give your chakras a cleanse, and attract even more things to be grateful for in life. Gratitude is an abundance magnet like you wouldn't believe! So, when you wake up in the morning—or whenever you wake

up, if you're a night owl—you should take the time to think about all the things you are thankful for in your life.

Feel appreciation for the lover in your bed or the fact that you've got a bed. Feel thankful for the food you'll eat, the great friends you have, and how you earn money. Feel thankful for all things, great and small. It helps to have a journal where you can list such things. Not a fan of journals? Then there's an app for you, some of which even offer daily reminders to make an entry.

8. *Use Crystals*: Crystals are like mother nature's version of a biofilter and batteries. They, as well as gemstones, can help your chakras resume their normal operations unimpeded so that Chi can flow through you, keeping you at ease, energetic, and in the flow. Consider using hematite for your root chakra, citrine for the solar plexus, rose quartz for your anahata, chrysocolla or lapis lazuli for your throat, sodalite to clear your third eye, and amethyst for your crown chakra.

9. *Get Colorful*: As mentioned, your chakras each have a color and vibration. Think of it as a rainbow of sorts, with a red root chakra, an orange sacral chakra, a yellow solar plexus, a green heart, a blue throat, an indigo thor eye, and a violet crown. To balance them, you can simply wear the colors that match each of these in the form of crystals, bangles, bracelets, clothing, and so on. You can also burn candles that match the chakra you want to balance out. Consider eating more foods that match that chakra color. You could also get a crystal bed lit up with various colors representing your chakras.

Chapter Four: The Practice of Meditation

There are many wrong ideas about meditation. For instance, most people think it is only about sitting still and remaining empty while doing their best to fight all the emotions and thoughts that bubble up within them. Meditation isn't about fighting your thoughts; what it's truly about is the focus. Meditation is a state of hyper-focus, where you consciously and deliberately place all your attention and awareness upon a singular point.

It is pertinent to note that there is nothing forceful about this practice. You do not force yourself to become empty of thoughts; that comes over time as you practice meditation.

A Brief History of Meditation

The most ancient concrete evidence about meditation can be found in the Indian subcontinent, specifically on the wall arts from about 5,000 to 3,500 BCE. These wall arts show people sitting in postures that are typical of the act of meditation with their eyes at half-mast. As far as writings on meditation go, the first is from around 1500 BCE, documented in the Vedas. Meditation has, for the longest time, been a practice of Hindus. According to the Upanishad, it is a great way to get rid of ignorance, build oneself in wisdom, and become one with the Divine.

Other forms of meditation came sometime around the sixth century to the fifth century BCE, in Buddhist India and China, where Taoism was practiced. There are writings about the various meditation levels in Indian Buddhism, particularly in Pali Canon's sutras, which are as old as the first century BCE. Pali Canon noted that meditation was one of the four steps that led to salvation, including respecting morals, contemplating truths, and acquiring knowledge. When Buddhism got to China, there was mention of enlightenment and Zen attained through meditation in the Vimalakirti Sutra passages from 100 CE.

Bodhidharma was the one responsible for sharing meditation to the Orient, bringing China the idea of Zen; however, Zhiyi was the one who founded the very first school in Central China during the sixth century. Zhiyi brought order to the teachings to be passed on in a way that was easy to assimilate.

Not to be disregarded, the Jews also had their practice, which they had inherited from older traditions. Among such practices is lasuach, which the Abrahamic patriarch Isaac practiced in the field, according to Genesis chapter 24, verse 63. In the Hebrew Bible (called the Tanakh), there are references to the act of meditating as well.

As Buddhism became popular in Japan from the seventh century, meditation was introduced to the country and developed further. In Nara, the first meditation hall in the country was opened by Dosho, a Japanese monk who first learned of Zen in 657 from China. Then the rules for Zazan were written by Dogen upon his return around 1227 from China to Japan. He garnered a monk community who focused on Zazen.

In Judaism, the practice evolved, and they included meditation in study, prayer, and mitzvot. They also included Kabbalah in their meditations and aspects of Jewish philosophy.

The Sufi philosophy, too, involves the act of meditation, called Dhikr, and includes "remembering God." It was a very important element of Sufism that took even deeper roots when it became more organized during the eleventh and twelfth centuries. During the latter part of this period, they had incorporated breathing methods and mantras.

Meditation in early Christianity was about repeating a certain phrase in a very particular posture. Its roots are found in the Byzantine period. Hesychasm, a mystical practice involving deep contemplation in prayer, was then developed in Greece on Mount Athos. Until now, it is still being practiced. It involves repeating The Prayer, or Jesus Prayer, "Lord Jesus Christ, Son of God, have mercy on me, a sinner." It's speculated that the Indians or the Sufis may have crossed paths with the Hesychasm practitioners—although there is no evidence of this.

In Western Christianity, the usual pillars of repetitive phrases or specific actions and postures are not a thing. From the sixth century, the closest thing to meditation among Western Christians was reading the Bible, a practice called the Lectio Divina, strictly adhered to by Benedictine monks. This practice was given more structure by Guigo II, a monk who lived in the twelfth century. According to him, it was a four-step process: lectio, meditatio, oratio, contemplatio, which means "read, ponder, pray, contemplate."

Through the latter part of the nineteenth century, meditation became very popular in the West thanks to the world becoming smaller on account of the internet and modern-day travel. Even the West has some of its meditation methodologies, which have spread to the East. In America, meditation became popular because of the presence of various European occult sects from 1840 to 1880. The 1893 World Parliament of Religions, which took place in Chicago, was also responsible for the growth in meditation's adoption in America. After that event, Swami Vivekananda went about setting up Vedanta ashrams. Then, there were lectures on Theravada Buddhist meditation, given by Anagarika Dharmapala in 1904, the Abdul Baha Bahai teaching tour, and Soyen Shaku, who focused on teaching Zen to Americans. By the 1890s, there were all sorts of new Yoga schools. Since then, meditation has continued to grow and thrive until now.

Learn All About Breathing

Breathing matters a lot in meditation. As you learn to control your breath, you learn to control other things. Breathe slow, and your heart rate goes down. Breathe fast, and it goes up. Breathe slow, and you are calm. Breathe fast, and you're either excited or anxious, depending on how you choose to interpret that energy. Breathing even affects how you digest your food. The more you practice conscious breathing, the more your body will benefit. You will keep better posture, relieve pain in your back from a misaligned spine, and strengthen your stomach muscles.

Are you breathing correctly? For a moment, put a hand on your chest. Rest it right on your breath bone. Take your other hand and put it on your stomach. Breathe how you usually do and do not change a thing. Notice your hands. If the hand or hands on your chest are moving, you're using the little muscles in between the ribs much more than usual. When you're seated, you don't need much oxygen compared to when you're moving about. So, you use these rib cage muscles instead of your abdomen. Since those muscles never get a day off, it's not the most efficient way to breathe.

Abdominal Breathing

1. First, keep your throat relaxed. Do this by opening your throat, which means you have to push your tongue downward a bit. Keep your mouth shut. The tongue position is temporary. You don't have to keep your tongue down all the time.

2. Next, note where the air goes when you breathe, whether it's your belly or lungs. Now, inhale by expanding your lungs, either by letting your belly or your chest swell. The air should flow in smoothly. Forget your nose. Just fill your lungs.

3. Next, exhale by compressing your belly or chest and let the air out. Forget about your nose. When you get used to this, you won't have to push your tongue down anymore.

4. Keep breathing until your breath becomes quiet and calm. You'll know you've made progress when you can do this without effort.

Embryonic Breathing

1. Breathe with your abdomen until your mind is quiet.

2. Next, invert your breathing. Note that this isn't comfortable at first. Focus on the area an inch or two beneath your navel.

3. On your inhale, draw in your navel as if you're exhaling. When you exhale, push out your navel as if you're inhaling. Continue to breathe this way.

4. When you're comfortable, focus on your lower back in addition to your stomach.

5. When you breathe, your belly will move inward on the inhale and outward on the exhale. This should be the same with your lower back. You will feel it if you're doing it right.

6. Think of your belly button and lower back as one, so you don't split your attention both ways.

Zen Meditation

This meditation involves being in the here and now, mindfully.

1. First, sit in a comfy position, keeping your back straight. If you're not okay with sitting cross-legged, you can use a chair. If you're sitting cross-legged, sit on a pillow, and make sure you're comfortable. Make sure your belly and chest are not

compressed. You may keep your hand on your knees or thighs.

2. Breathe in, pulling the air into you with your stomach. With each exhale, relax your shoulders. As you breathe in, feel yourself breathing in good prana that fills you with life and all good things. Release the bad, problems, and stress with each exhale.

3. Now that you're even more relaxed, focus inside. When you breathe in, in your mind, say, "Here." Listen to that word and be more attentive to what it means. You're where you are, which is here.

4. Exhale and release that thought. Then inhale and hear "here" in your mind again. Here, on the floor or table. Exhale and release the thought. Meditate on "here" for about five breaths, but no more than ten. Don't be in a hurry.

5. When you feel even more grounded than when you started—meaning more aware of your here-ness—continue to hear "here" on the inhale, but add "now" on the exhale. Think about what now means—the current moment.

6. Continue to inhale on here and exhale on now, contemplating the meaning of each one. You should feel very aware of your existence. You should now be in the state of I Am.

7. As a standalone practice, you can continue with this for ten minutes, fifteen tops. To get ready for Zazen, you'll want to do this for no more than five minutes.

Please keep in mind that the goal here is not an empty mind but an aware one. It might help to have a gentle smile on your face as you practice so that you do not get upset or irritated at all the distracting thoughts that will pop up. There is no need to force yourself to be thoughtless. The goal is to set your mind free of worries and be here, now.

Sit in Zazen

From the previous technique, you flow into this one. It is simple, but do not be fooled. It will plunge you into the deepest ocean of awareness.

1. Sit comfy, back straight, preferably with crossed legs on a little pillow, or one high enough to keep your posture upright. Don't sit cross-legged if you can't hold that position too long. Use a chair (if this is you), but ideally, you should practice sitting cross-legged daily. If the place is noisy, try to find somewhere silent, and put on calming music.

2. Rest your hands on your laps with your palms facing up. Let your right hand cover your left underneath, partially. Your thumbs should touch just above your hands, creating an oval. This is the cosmic mudra or hand position, which should be positioned just below your navel. This allows your focus to remain there in addition to your breath. This position beneath and just behind your belly button is called the garden of energy, or Dantien.

3. You may shut your eyes if you're just starting, but you can leave them open or even half-open in the traditional method. More advanced practitioners tend to keep their eyes open so they remain aware and don't fall asleep. If you keep your eyes open or halfway shut, find a point not too far off in front of you to gaze at on the floor. If you shut your eyes and you feel like you're drifting, open them again to reground yourself in the now.

4. Breathe abdominally. Don't try to control your breath in any way. Just make sure your lungs and belly are pulling in air, not your nose.

5. Notice your breath. Don't try to change it. Notice as it changes on its own.

6. Now focus on your nose as the air enters your nostrils or focus just beneath your navel as it goes up and down. Visualize the airflow through your nose, through your lungs, to your Dantien, and out again.

7. Now count your breath. One breath consists of either the inhale or exhale. So, breathe in . . . one, breathe out . . . two, breathe in . . . three, breathe out . . . four. Continue until you hit ten (an exhale) and then begin again at one (an inhale). If you miss a count, just start over, and don't worry about it. Be patient and gentle with yourself.

8. Let any images or thoughts pop up. Don't try to suppress them. Let them come and go, and don't linger. With time, the noise will cease. The way to let go is not to try to let go. Just come back to your breath every time you notice you've wandered off. Continue to count your breath until ten and then restart.

9. Certain thoughts are more persistent than others and continue to return. This doesn't mean you're failing. Don't fight the thoughts. Allow them to make a home in your mind, just for a bit so that you can observe them, but make sure you remain aware of your breath so the thoughts don't take over your mind. When they're losing energy, you can release them and fully return to counting to ten. Release all thoughts with a loving, gentle smile so you don't get frustrated and distracted.

10. You might find that you've moved your awareness from your breath to your counting alone. In that case, come back to the breath. The counting is a tool, not the main goal.

11. If you've been able to count from one to ten and haven't gotten distracted (something that might happen on your first day of practice or your fifty-first . . . There's no rushing this), you can now make each count encompass both the inhale and exhale. In other words, breathe in and out, and that's one. Breathe in, then out, and that's two, and so on.

12. The more you practice (not in one sitting but over several sessions), the better your concentration will become, and you will be able to focus on the breath without counting. When you notice you're losing concentration, you may count and then stop when you feel you're fully on your breath again.

13. Soon, you'll be in Zazen. At this point, your only job is to observe the silence within you while remaining aware of your breath. You may receive mind-blowing revelations. They will differ from person to person, so practice finding out and remember to be patient.

Mantra Meditation

This involves repeating your mantra over and over until you hit the state of consciousness that you should. It is repeating the words until they lose meaning, leading you to the same place as Zen. Choose a mantra whose meaning you understand; better still, pick one in a language you understand. Not using Sanskrit does not mean your practice will be weak. After all, this practice's originators understood their language, and so the Sanskrit mantras had deep meanings for them.

If you insist on using a mantra, OM or AUM is an easy one and one of the oldest. It represents the universe and your connection to it and the powers that control it. You may practice with this mantra by saying it out loud or intoning on the inside, with no external sound. You can either pronounce it "Ooommm," giving equal time to both the O and the M, or you could go, "Ommmmm," with more time spent on the M, or "Oooooooommm," with more time spent on the O. It doesn't matter. Find what works for you.

Om on the Inside

1. Wear comfy, loose clothing. Sit in a comfy, cross-legged position, hands on your thighs, palms up, forefinger and thumb lightly touching, while you stretch out your other fingers as they rest on your thigh. This hand position is the chin mudra.

2. Shut your eyes, breathe regularly with your abdomen.

3. Begin to repeat the mantra in your mind at your own pace, allowing it to flow naturally. Keep your attention on the mantra, not the breathing. If you're comfortable breathing properly without much thought, you can do as you like.

4. Whether slow or fast, let Om ring out clearly in your mind. You can match it to your heartbeat or your breath. You can chant it internally on each inhale and exhale, or you can chant it several times per breath. You could chant it only on exhales or inhales. Do what feels right. You will slow down the pace naturally after a few minutes and begin to develop a rhythm. Don't force this, as it will happen on its own.

Chanting Om Out Loud

The same instructions apply from chanting internally, except that you can only chant the Om on the exhale, and you should not pause in between the in-breath and out-breath. Don't try to control how you breathe. Let the Om flow in a low, consistent voice for as long as your breath will allow.

Soon, the chanting will grow longer, in both breath and frequency. Your body will begin to vibrate, and you will sense this in your skill, mouth, teeth, tongue, and chest, as well as all over your head. This vibration then moves over to your mind, and your thoughts will calm down. Your emotions will also even out.

Qigong Meditation

Qigong (or Chi King) involves harnessing your Chi or Qi, your internal energy and life force. Qi is the essence of life. It flows through your veins and lymph. It is the air you breathe, the energy used to digest food, and the energy you get from food. It's the electric charges and impulses that flow through all your cells and your brain. It's part of everything that works to keep you living and breathing, whether physical or nonphysical.

The essence of this meditation is to help your awareness of your Qi grow, so you can harness it and channel it where it's needed. It also serves to enlighten you spiritually by redirecting the energy from your belly to your brain.

1. Sit crossed-legged and put your hands in the mudra position. You may sit on a chair if sitting with your legs crossed is uncomfortable. Keep your back straight and begin with abdominal breathing. You may begin with Zazen.

2. Make sure your tongue is resting against the upper palate. The best position is the one your tongue fits into naturally. Your teeth and mouth should be shut, but not tightly so. This tongue position matters a lot, as it helps you intensify your meditation. It's okay to swallow if you need to.

3. To sense your Qi, breathe embryonically. If you cannot breathe this way yet, breathe abdominally. Do make a point to master embryonic breathing, as this is the traditional breathing method for Qigong.

4. Be aware of your Dantien (the spot just below and behind your navel).

5. If you struggle with concentration, you may count your breaths from one to ten and then resume the count again until you're focused.

6. Any thoughts that pop up should be allowed to pass. Don't linger.

7. Continue to observe your Dantien as it moves with each inhale and exhale. It generates new energy with each compression of the in-breath and expansion of the out-breath. Notice the Dantien, and you will begin to feel this energy. Please do not rush this or force it. Just be patient.

Chapter Five: Mystical Breathwork

As mentioned, breathing is very central to all meditative practices. There are all sorts of breathing techniques that can help you in your practice, and two of the important ones have already been covered. Breathing done right can take you to unimaginable heights, and you only need to give it a try to prove it. You may find that you have severely underestimated your lungs all this time.

Breathing does more than keep you alive. Spiritually, breathing the right way can lead you to higher states of consciousness where all illusions fall apart, and you see the truth of all existence. It is interesting to note that in many old languages—from Aramaic, Latin, Tibetan, Greek, and Latin, to Hawaiian, Amazonian Quechua, and Andean Quechua—breath means spirit, life, and soul.

Why should you learn breathwork? Here are seven good reasons to spur you on:

- To grow in consciousness
- To gain insight
- To attain deep healing

- To receive vision and clarity on your life

- To recharge your body

- To remove all stress

- To connect with your spirit guides

A Better Understanding of Breathwork

This is a very ancient practice that began in the 1970s. It is about being conscious about how you breathe and deliberately directing your breath. The goal is to improve your physical health, transform you completely, and connect you with the mystical.

You could practice so many forms of breathwork, with some of them being as old as pranayama and others being as recent as the Wim Hof breathing method. Breathwork is amazing because it has a relaxing effect on your nervous system. It also teaches you to accept yourself, alleviates depression, improves your immunity, keeps your blood alkaline, reduces inflammation, enhances clear thought, and gives you more focus. It increases your vitality and energy, leads to happiness and joy, boosts your creativity, helps you connect with others better, leads to spiritual insights and mystical experiences, and boosts your awareness.

Different Kinds of Breathwork

- *Pranayama*: The oldest form, meaning "breath control," is made up of techniques that let you free up the flow of prana and boost your self-realization regarding spiritual development. You can practice this on its own or along with yoga. There are eight kinds of pranayama, but the most common ones are the Alternate Nostril Breathing (known as Nadi Shodhan), the Skull Shining Breath (called Kapalabjati), and the Conqueror Breath (also called Ujjayi).

• *Rebirthing Breathwork*: This was created in the 70s by Leonard Orr. He had reportedly experienced his birth again in a bathtub, which was how he came up with this breathwork method. The point of this method is to create a connection between you and your subconscious so that you can let go of any childhood trauma that still holds you back and go through a rebirth that gives you life and sets you free. The way to do this breathwork is with circular breathing, and it helps if you have someone who is trained in this method to be with you. Sometimes, this breathwork will take place in a bathtub, so you can have the experience of being born again.

• *Holotropic Breathwork*: This was created by Christina and Stanislav Grof, both Czech psychiatrists. They also created this back in the 70s to help others experience true transformation and healing on an inner level. The Grof's were inspired by their study and experience of the astounding effects of LSD, so they developed this after the drug was banned in the 1960s. They wanted to find a way to recreate the effects of LSD naturally without having to worry about legal prohibitions and the side effects of drug use. To practice this method, you need primal, rhythmical music and to breathe as fast as you can for two hours at least. In the end, you draw mandalas with other participants and talk about your experiences. This is a technique that is best overseen by a professional practitioner.

• *Wim Hof Breathwork*: A new method founded on the principles of pranayamic methods. Wim Hof, an extreme athlete from the Netherlands, developed it—a man also called the Iceman because of his ability to feel at home with ridiculously cold temperatures and ice baths for extended periods. For him, you must expose yourself to the cold, hyperventilate in a controlled way, and meditate. You will need to take thirty power breaths, breathe in deeply, and then hold your breath for as long as you can. When you can no longer do so, exhale, and then inhale deeply for ten to fifteen seconds, after which you can exhale. Do this same process three more times.

- *Shamanic Breathwork*: A modern take on the old circular breathing method meant to connect you with the shaman within you. Linda Star Wolf, a shaman and teacher, developed this method in the 1990s. The process begins with smudging, chanting, and then setting intentions. After that, you must breathe in a rhythm to primal music, like drums. Some practitioners also include practices like contacting your spirit animal and healing your chakra during breathwork. Besides getting in touch with the shaman within you, you will also experience healing, get guidance from within, and feel more whole.

Your Path to Spiritual Growth

Breathwork can lead to great spiritual heights. It is important that before you begin each session, you make your intentions very clear. If you do not have a clear intention, you might not notice any concrete changes that happen on account of your practice.

You must begin by considering the one thing you are having the most difficulty with in life now, whether it is a relationship, your health, finances, or your career. Breathwork can help you with whatever you're dealing with, not just by getting rid of the surface symptoms but by getting to the very heart of the matter—this is often rooted in the spirit.

Breathwork is a useful tool for altering your consciousness and connecting with the divine without relying on drugs. You can use it to connect with the spirit world so that you can find the most amazing discoveries, both about specific issues in your life and life as a whole. You only need to select the best form of breathwork for you so that you can reap the benefits of the process. This is how you release all the pain and trauma that have remained trapped in you, holding you down and keeping you from growing to great spiritual heights.

Practicing Breathwork

Before you proceed with this breathwork, you should make sure that you (and anyone else practicing with you) does not have a history of high blood pressure, aneurysms, cardiovascular disease, glaucoma, or retinal detachment. You also should exercise caution if you've had surgery or any recent injury to your body. Pregnant women should also not engage in this breathwork.

As you practice, you will feel all sorts of emotions. You could feel serene, meditative, sleepy, joyful, or deeply relaxed. You might even find yourself shedding tears as you let go of old trauma. Some people have even experienced a few of their past lives too. It is best to do this with someone who knows what you're up to and will help you if you need something. Finally, know that you can stop at any time.

1. First, set up your space. You'll want a yoga mat. Some people place a pillow beneath their heads and a rolled-up blanket or another pillow beneath their knees. You could also use another blanket to keep you warm in case you get cold.

2. Do not go beyond twenty minutes. When you're done, bring your breath back to its baseline and take ten minutes afterward to relax while lying down. Make sure you have a timer. Having a partner also helps.

3. Lie on your back. Set the pillows and blankets up in a way so that you're comfy. Shut your eyes and relax for a few minutes.

4. Breathe in deep and slow abdominally. Once you have gotten to the endpoint of your inhale, exhale right away at the same speed. When you're at the endpoint of your exhale, immediately inhale again, keeping it slow, steady, and deep. This is circular breathing.

5. As you breathe, remain mindful, and never hold your breath. When your lungs are almost filled with air, start your exhale, and when they're almost empty, start your inhale.

6. You'll find that your breathing wants to get faster, but don't let it, because if you do, you will generate tension in your body. Keep your body and lungs nice and relaxed, so you can continue breathing this way for a long while.

7. For emotional release, you'll want to inhale and exhale with your mouth. If you're more comfortable using your nose, that's fine. After about ten minutes, your body will settle into its rhythm. You will notice your extremities are tingling. You'll probably feel euphoric and like you're in a different state of consciousness.

8. Once the twenty minutes are up, your partner should gently touch you on the shoulder, so you can begin to bring your breath gently back to its regular rhythm. Notice what you've learned and how that connects with your present reality. If you don't have a partner, make sure your alarm is a soft tone that lightly brings you out of your practice.

Alternate Nostril Breathing

Alternate nostril breathing is also called Nadi Shodhana. It is a pranayama technique that allows you to discover inner peace. If you deal with a lot of stress, this is the practice to get your life back. It also does wonders when you do not feel very grounded or when you are having trouble sleeping.

With alternate nostril breathing, you can gain mental clarity and amp up your focus. It also helps your body get rid of toxins, clear all energy channels, and balances both hemispheres of your brain.

1. Sit in a comfy position, with your legs crossed and your bottom supported by a cushion.

2. Leave your left hand resting upon your left knee.

3. Raise your right hand to your nose.

4. Exhale until your lungs are empty, and then shut your right nostril with your right thumb.

5. Breathe in through your left nostril and then close that same nostril with your fingers.

6. Open your right nostril and breathe out from it.

7. Now, breathe in through your right nostril and then cover it with your thumb.

8. Open your left nostril and then breathe out through it. You have just completed one cycle of alternate nostril breathing.

9. Keep this up for five minutes, and make sure you always end each session by breathing out through the left nostril.

You can practice this anytime you like, wherever you are, if you feel comfortable. If you like, you can do it in the morning, evening, or both times. You can also use this to relax or focus. Ideally, this practice is best done when your stomach is empty. You do not want to do this when you are ill or when your airways are congested.

Try doing this before or after you do yoga and see how that works out for you. You might find that your meditation becomes even deeper and richer because of incorporating this practice.

The 4-7-8 Breathing Method

If you ever find yourself in dire need of good sleep or want to get a handle on your emotions or cravings and reduce anxiety, this is the method to use. It is also a great option when you do not have enough time to get into a really deep breathwork practice. It allows you to get in touch with your body and feelings and gives your nervous system a much-needed break.

1. Sit somewhere comfy, cross-legged, and shut your eyes. Part your lips slightly.

2. Inhale through the nose for four counts.

3. Hold your breath for seven counts.

4. Breathe out through your slightly parted lips for eight counts.

Soft Belly Breathing Method

Sadly, many people breathe only using the chest. They do not get those good, belly-deep breaths unless they are yawning or drowning in sweat in the middle of a Shaun T workout. The thing about breathing with your chest instead of your belly is that it causes stress and tension and makes your mind restless. When you breathe from your belly, it centers you. That said, a lot of people get involved in belly breathing and make it hard work, forgetting one vital thing: You must keep it soft! Using force will only cause more anxiety and tension—exactly what you don't need during your practice.

When your belly is soft during breathwork, your vagus nerve is activated. The nerve moves through your belly and chest to your central nervous system, terminating at your brain. This nerve stimulation will help your body relax, slow your heart rate, improve your blood pressure and digestion, and relax your muscles and mind. Your amygdala will also calm down a bit, which is great because this is the part of the brain that makes you angry and fearful. The vagus nerve is the answer to the fight-freeze-flight conundrum people face in stressful situations.

Your vagus nerve has a branch that connects with parts of your brain that make it easier for you to connect with people around you and form bonds, so as you breathe as deeply and slowly as you can, stimulating your vagus nerve, you inevitably will improve your relationships with others as a result.

Let go of all thoughts that say you need to be forceful about your breath when you are practicing this one. The case with this method is that less is more. So, take it easy. Imagine if you will a cloud, soft, not resisting the winds. This is what you want your stomach to feel like. Often, people clench their abs in defense against threats, whether physical or verbal. This immediately puts you on the offense or defense, which is counterproductive to the whole practice of breathwork. When you're in this position, you cannot reap the spiritual and physical benefits of soft belly breathing. So, do your best to let go of your gut and allow it just to be. If you're in the habit of sucking your gut in so you look better in clothes, wear loose clothes for this one, and do this by yourself so that you don't feel self-conscious about how you look.

1. Sit comfortably, legs crossed, your eyes shut.

2. Let your stomach relax and become soft. The softer you keep it, the more air goes into your lungs, allowing your body to benefit from extra oxygen.

3. Just breathe abdominally, making sure your stomach stays nice and soft.

4. As you breathe, allow the relaxation in your stomach to spread to the rest of your body.

5. With each breath, allow your body to sink even deeper and deeper into relaxation.

Whatever you do, do not do this practice right after a meal as you will fall asleep. You can do this if you have trouble falling asleep. If you are using it to go to bed at night, you will not need a timer. At any other time, you want to do this for just five to ten minutes each time.

Visualization Breathing

There are so many ways to visualize while doing breathwork. You can use whatever visualization you need that matches you and your personality. Here are your options:

- Visualize each chakra as you breathe prana into them.

- Visualize your entire body being washed over by light as you breathe in and out.

- Visualize inhaling light, and exhaling darkness, until all you are is light.

- Visualize air going in, around, and out of your respiratory system.

- Visualize illness and anxiety leaving your body on every exhale.

- Visualize breathing in someone else's pain and then exhaling loving-kindness toward them instead. This is Tonglen, which is a Buddhist practice.

Triangle Breathwork

Triangle breathing is the absolute best for dealing with anxiety and panic attacks. The reason it works so well is that it is more about a longer exhale.

1. Sit in a comfy position in a quiet place.

2. Breathe in for four counts.

3. Hold that breath for four seconds.

4. Breathe out for a count of six.

5. Resume the cycle again, the whole time visualizing a triangle. Move from one point of the triangle to the next with each breath.

Square Breathwork

This is almost the same thing as the triangle method. If you are not great at memorizing techniques, you can focus on this one. It is also a good one for kids to practice.

1. Get comfy in a seated position and make sure there are no distractions.

2. Inhale for four counts.

3. Hold that breath for four counts.

4. Breathe out for four counts.

5. As you breathe in and out, visualize a square. You can move from point to point on each inhale, hold, and exhale.

Chapter Six: Inducing Deeper Mystical States

Most people go through life without realizing that there are all sorts of states of consciousness for you to perceive. A number of those tend to experience the altered states of consciousness by using illegal drugs and harmful substances—which are not endorsed by this book. The good news is that there are ways to experience life from a different focus or state of consciousness without putting harmful substances into your body. Before you investigate ways to experience the mystical, you need to learn about the various states.

Trance

Mystical experiences will often fall into a category based on what they are about and the state of consciousness experienced. A trance state is one where the psychic reigns supreme. In this state, you only need to think about something to obtain results that ordinarily can only be gotten by using action or willpower.

The deeper you fall into a trance, the more you lose the perceptions that come from your regular senses until all that is left is the world of the psychic. Your five senses are very inhibited regarding what they can perceive of the world of trance—and for a good reason. They were designed to help you see the physical world, not the psychic one. For this same reason, science finds it extremely difficult to accept the reality of trance as the curious result of chemicals and neurons *and* as an actual reality. Science makes the mistake of assuming that physical instruments designed to give feedback to physical senses would register the reality of other states of consciousness that are anything but physical.

In a trance state, your physical perceptions are limited, which allows you to take a deep dive into the world from that perspective with no inhibitions or conflicts, so you can see things that would ordinarily be troublesome if you encountered them in your "normal" state of mind, without freaking out. When in a trance, it takes a trained mind to be aware of being in one, just like you would need practice before being aware that you're in a dream. In a trance state, even your daydreams take on the quality of being real.

Reverie

When you are in a reverie, many mystical events happen without your consciousness being inhibited in any way. This means that you see whatever happens more as a revelation than as a reality. The visions you get are usually pure allegory and will need to be properly interpreted to understand the meaning of what you see.

Dreams

Dreams also count as mystical experiences. Some dream of the future or perceived warnings and revelations when they go off into la-la land. Dreams are as old as civilization and have often served as premonitions of the future, bringers of divine insight and messages, and doorways to parts of consciousness that you could never explore any other way. They are a lot more than just "brain cells winding down after a hard day's work." Dreams occur in a state of consciousness that is not physical. You can consider them a whole world of their own, offering a gateway to other states of consciousness to the adept, who know how to dream effectively.

Near-Death Experiences (NDEs)

This is a valid state of consciousness, which, as implied, happens when one is at the precipice of death. This is not to encourage suicide or becoming an accomplice to murder; it happens to those who survive death, with many describing it as leaving this world for another. Some accounts prove that the world is indeed multidimensional, and there is more to life than meets the eye. Again, do not try to induce this type of mystical experience.

Out-of-Body Experiences (OOBEs)

Also known as astral projection, this is a state of consciousness and mystical experience that involves moving your awareness from the physical to the astral plane. This often happens through deliberate methods—although it can happen spontaneously as well. In astral projection, you project your consciousness from your physical body to your astral body. Often, this is experienced as stepping out of, floating, or pulling away from your physical body as it sleeps—though, in the grand scheme of things, that is not the case.

Your astral body is not leaving your physical body—though that process is the interpretation your mind gives it. What is happening is that you are a multidimensional being who spends most of their time focused on the physical plane, so when you experience astral projection, you are simply moving that focus to the astral plane. This is something you already do every night—although if you're not an experienced projector, you either forget you did it, or you spend your time chasing the seeming randomness of whatever dreamlike experience you find yourself in.

You can deliberately induce this state by concentrating in a "mind awake, body asleep" fashion on the desire to project and pulling your astral body out of your physical, like how a ghost leaves a body in old-timey films. In your astral body, you can visit places on Earth and beyond. You can discover new worlds, check out the Akashic records, and even influence your physical life from that plane to receive healing, success, inspiration, and more.

Five Levels of Trance

You will learn more detail about trance states by covering the five levels of trance.

First Level: Ultralight Trance — In this trance stage, you become very aware of what's going on in your mind. You become aware of what you are thinking and feeling, both in terms of sensation and emotion. You tend to enter this stage of trance when you're practicing mindful meditation.

Second Level: Light Trance — At this stage, it's almost like a dream. You get lost in your fantasy or whatever you are daydreaming about. When you're watching Netflix, or listening to a podcast, or driving down a very familiar route, you're in a state of light trance.

Third Level: Medium Trance — In this state, you feel like you are "in the zone." This is called the flow state, where you lose track of time—and your bodily needs. You don't remember that you've got to eat or go to the bathroom. This happens when you're immersed in very creative work that you're enjoying or when you're taking part in an activity that thrills you endlessly.

Fourth Level: Deep Trance — Not to be confused with your Spotify playlist, this is the level of trance that happens when you are asleep and experiencing hypnagogia, which is when images begin to form on the blank screen of your shut eyes just before dreams. This state is often fleeting, and it takes practice to hold on to it. It starts with weird, swirling colors and shapes and then moves on to creating weird images that are the makings of a dream. Sometimes, this can be accompanied by feelings of being touched, or even sounds—like someone singing, laughing, your name, or a conversation you're eavesdropping on.

Fifth Level: Ultra-Deep Trance — In this stage, you have no consciousness at all. It is the same as being asleep with your brain in the delta state, where it's deep and dreamless. If you want to do any mystical or spiritual work, it goes without saying that you want to be at any level from two to four.

Different Ways to Alter Your Consciousness

Method #1: Meditation — By now, you know that meditation is about sitting quietly and being mindfully in the here and now. Here is how to use it to alter your state of consciousness.

1. Sit in a comfy position in a quiet place where you can get at least thirty minutes of peace. You may sit in a chair or sit with your legs crossed in a lotus position if it's comfortable for you. If using a chair, keep your spine ramrod straight, but remain relaxed, not rigid.

2. Set your hands upon your lap, folded. You can put your hands in your preferred mudra or simply have your palms facing upward to allow energy to flow into and through you.

3. Sit in silence for fifteen to twenty minutes. The more experience you get, the longer you can sit.

4. Keep your eyes open if you're prone to drifting off to sleep during your practice. Keep your gaze on the spot on the floor just a few feet ahead. Don't stare; just let your eyes rest on the spot. You should be seeing without really looking at it. Then, point your awareness inside.

5. As you meditate, you will notice that your concentration and focus continue to improve—if not in a session, over several sessions. Don't force it.

6. You may chant the OM mantra or any other mantra you want to. If you prefer, you can begin by counting to center yourself.

Method #2: Observation — With this method, you're going to just stare at something and then stick with it no matter what. It's really easy to attain another state of consciousness without using drugs here. For the most part, people tend to experience a lot of altered consciousness through the sense of sight, but you can easily experience this with your other senses.

1. Pick an object, like a small ball, flower, or spoon.

2. Take that object to a place where you can be at ease and not distracted or bothered.

3. Relax and put yourself in a state of mind where the only thing that you care about is that object in your hand.

4. Hold the object up in front of your eyes, about six inches away, or as close as you can to have a sharp focus on it.

5. Now, look at this object, and continue to do so. This is the challenge: STICK WITH IT.

6. You should do your best not to blink. Yes, you will blink, but do your best to make sure that you have long periods where you don't, so your focus on your chosen object remains unbroken.

7. Don't move around, no matter how much you want to. Just keep your eyes locked on the object.

8. When five minutes have gone by, you will notice that there have been some changes to the object and its background. Where the spoon ends and the background begins will blur.

9. You'll also notice that any objects in the background will begin to fuzz out and look weird. Continue to focus, and you might notice some movement and even faces.

Please note that you should use something small, which will give you a lot of background space to work with. You could use a white piece of paper. Another version of this is simply you staring at your reflection in the mirror without blinking. You could also try this with someone else, staring at them instead. You will both experience an altered state of consciousness at the same time. Just make sure you pick a partner who respects the mystical, is comfortable with you, and won't spontaneously burst into laughter because they are not taking the practice seriously.

Method #3: The Dervish Whirl — You might be worried about hurling or something, but you will be fine. There is nothing dangerous about spinning when you do it right.

1. Go outside. Find somewhere beautiful with soft ground so that you can fall safely. Make sure there's nothing close to you that could hurt you.

2. Stand in a spot and be still for a moment, with your eyes shut.

3. Now, begin to spin counterclockwise, no matter what your dominant hand is.

4. Use one foot to push you off the floor and the other one to give you balance.

5. You may spin like the Sufis do, with your hands held out just like wings, your right fingers pointed upward to allow energy from above, and your left fingers pointed downward to share that energy with all around you.

6. As you spin, take note of your heartbeat. Really feel it.

7. Visualize or feel your heart generating deep, powerful mystical energy.

8. If you happen to fall, just get up again and keep on spinning.

9. If you find that you cannot continue, just stop and allow yourself to lie on the floor in a corpse pose or savasana, on your back, arms pointing down and away from the body, legs spread out. You can open your eyes if you want to now. If it feels too intense, keep them closed and feel the energy from the earth grounding you.

Method #4: Self-Hypnosis — This is an easy one. You will need an object to focus on to hypnotize yourself. You can use anything but consider using a candle.

1. Take your candle somewhere no one will bother you, and then light it.

2. Pick a phrase, mantra, or keyword that you will use to hypnotize yourself. It could be any of the following: *Deeper, lower, slower, further, more, now, heavy, I'm going deeper, I'm more relaxed,* or *my trance is deeper and deeper.* The goal is to convince yourself that you're now entranced.

3. You may lie or sit down and then look at your candle. You don't have to stare at it for long intervals. It's only there to center you so that you can move from normal waking awareness to trance.

4. As you look at the flame, instruct yourself along these lines: "I'm getting sleepy . . . So sleepy. My eyes are getting heavy . . . heavier with each breath. I'm slipping down, down, and away. My eyes are drooping shut . . . It's hard to keep them open." As you instruct yourself this way, make sure that you're taking nice, deep belly breaths.

5. As your eyes begin to shut, you're on the precipice of being in a state of hypnosis. This is when you should use your keyword or phrase from step two. This way, your trance grows deeper. Hold onto your keyword, repeating it over and over, allowing it to take you even deeper.

6. You must relax at this point. As you say your keyword, move your consciousness around your body, scanning it for tension. Begin from the top of your head, moving slowly down your face, neck, and so on. Whenever you find a tense spot, pause there, relax it, and then move on. Keep this up until your body is relaxed, and your trance will become even deeper.

7. Now it's time to count yourself down, going from ten to one. While counting, feel yourself going even deeper and further into your inner self. Allow your eyes to droop with weight.

8. Focus on each part of your body again. This time, you should feel your body becoming heavier and heavier. All your limbs should be heavy.

9. Next, you want to remove the weight from your limbs so that they feel like clouds floating. You feel like you're floating up and away, going deeper, higher, further.

10. If you're ready to come out of this state, simply instruct yourself by saying, "I will now finish my trance and come back up." When you come out of it, you'll notice you feel energized, refreshed, and ready for whatever.

This is an amazing tool to use when you want to be better at concentration, get rid of bad habits, or banish insomnia. You must keep in mind that if you are skeptical or have bad expectations from the onset, this will ruin your results. You also want to make sure you are relaxed because if you're not, you won't get great results either. Expect great results, be relaxed, stay positive, and you will enjoy your self-hypnosis session.

Method#5: Nonstop Singing — This method involves a particular melody using various frequencies. It works the same way chanting does, changing your breathing pattern and creating vibrations within you.

1. Say "Ah." Open your mouth widely as though you're about to get a dental exam.

2. Begin by saying "Ah" out loud, forcefully.

3. Turn that "Ah" into a melody and continue to sing it. Don't bother about how great or terrible you sound—the goal is to keep on singing.

4. Change the tones of your "Ah" song from high to low and play around with the intensity.

5. Do this for twenty minutes, and you should enter an altered state.

Method #6: Fasting— There are many kinds of fasts, but the whole point behind them is abstinence from food and sometimes water, as in the case of a dry fast. Fasting is a very healthy thing to do, but you must never do this without medical supervision. It helps to cleanse your body and give you clarity of mind.

You may not know this, but it is possible to go for days without food and longer than three days without water. An extended dry fast—lasting more than one day—is much more dangerous than a fast in which you can drink water, so please do not engage in this without medical supervision. Furthermore, dry fasting is best left to the experienced fasters. If you have an eating disorder, please do not use this method to alter your state of consciousness. You should only fast if you're of sound health in body and mind.

1. Begin by learning to eat just twice a day, especially if you always have three square meals a day. You can skip breakfast, and you won't suffer for it, contrary to the lie propagated by breakfast cereal companies about how "it's the most important meal of the day!" It isn't.

2. Once you're used to eating twice, move on to eating one meal a day, which is called OMAD fasting.

3. When you are used to that, you want to add on time gradually. Fast for twenty-four hours, and then when you're used to that, try 48-hour fasts.

4. Always come off your fast by refeeding lightly on some easy to digest fish and veggies, with a small serving of fruit.

5. When you're used to 48's, try a three-day fast. It usually takes about three days for all hunger to disappear, and then there will be a white film on your tongue. This is normal.

When you hit the 72-hour mark, you will often feel a different state of mind. You'll be very clear about your life, clearer than you have ever been. Your mind moves fast. Your sense of sight and smell are heightened ridiculously, like those of a hunter seeking prey to kill and eat. You become aware of your shortcomings in life and what you need to do to change them so that you can move ahead. If you can fast, absolutely try it. You will have no regrets and a flattering figure! Make sure you do not engage in any strenuous activity and don't have much to do during your fasts so that you can get optimal results. Also, refeed correctly so that you don't pass out or give yourself diarrhea.

Speaking of runny stomachs . . . When you are fasting, never, EVER trust your wind. Assume it is something with a bit more *substance.* Then, find a bathroom to make doubly sure. If you're feeling tuckered out before you hit the 72-hour mark, make sure you get electrolytes with no frills. Check out the Snake Diet electrolyte powder mix, which is very convenient to use. Electrolytes will give you energy during your fast. If you cannot get any, just get some pink Himalayan salt or regular salt to snack on.

Method #7: Chanting Mantras — Chanting can get you to an altered state easily, with awesome results. As you chant, you will also learn better breath control and infuse your body with more oxygen. According to Bernard Aaronson, you can chant your name, drawing out each syllable, and then pausing to take a breath before you repeat it. If you prefer, you could stick with mantras like the popular, powerful OM or the chakra mantras.

1. Sit comfortably in a place where you won't be disturbed for 35 minutes.

2. Shut your eyes, focus on your base chakra, and chant LUM for the next five minutes, breathing deeply in between each chant and expelling all inhaled breath with the chant. Feel the energy in this chakra.

3. Next, move the energy from your root chakra upward as you chant VUM for the next five minutes, focusing on the sacral chakra.

4. Chant RUM for five minutes, with your awareness at your solar plexus chakra.

5. Chant YUM for five minutes as you focus on your heart chakra.

6. Chant HUM for five minutes and keep your awareness on your throat chakra.

7. Chant OM for five minutes and focus on your third eye chakra.

8. Now be aware of your crown chakra as you sit in silence for five minutes, breathing deeply.

9. Remember to move the energy up through your spine, through each chakra, and let it all arrive at your head.

Chapter Seven: Developing Psychic Abilities — Opening Your Third Eye

Your third eye chakra is right on your forehead, just above and in between your eyebrows. It is called the Ajna (or Dvidak Padma). It's responsible for intuition and foresight, and it works when you allow yourself to be open and engage with your imagination constantly. According to Yoga metaphysics, it is the midpoint of your "I" persona, which is set apart from everyone else in the world. Its color is purple, and it's reminiscent of moonlight.

The symbol of this chakra is the Om. Krishna, the God of Wisdom in Hinduism, oversees this chakra. When you chant Om, you are stimulating the Ajna, which helps you focus, grounds you, and makes you realize the Divinity within all of life—little wonder, as the Om is the seed from which all the creation sprouts.

Also, within the symbol is an upside-down triangle and the lotus flower, representing wisdom. The triangle is a depiction of wisdom in bloom, as it grows within you. It represents the broadening of your insight, which brings you closer and closer to spiritual enlightenment. As for the lotus flower, it is connected to Brahma, the God of

Creation in Hinduism. It depicts the beauty of life, fertility, prosperity in all your affairs, and eternity. Ajna is a chakra that is made up of indigo hues and deep blue and violet shades. When these colors are put together, they communicate mystery, wisdom, faith, loyalty, and royalty.

This chakra is connected to your pineal gland, which is shaped like a little pine cone and is in your brain. It is responsible for creating melatonin in your body, which is why you can sleep and wake up at the right time, assuming you listen to your body.

When your Ajna is out of balance, you cannot see clearly, and you have a hard time thinking with clarity. Anything spiritual or mystical, you reject out of hand. You cannot see what the big picture is and become so fixated on little details that it's hard to have faith and trust that things will work out.

When it is a little too active, your Ajna gets no support from the other chakras, so you get lost in a world of illusion and mere fantasy. You have problems clarifying where you want to go in life since you have no vision with your chakra out of whack. Therefore, you must make sure this chakra remains balanced at all times. When it's imbalanced, you are out of touch with reality and closer to winding up in a straight jacket, the longer you let that happen. As much as the physical world is illusory, you're here and a part of it, and so it would be wise to honor it as a reality of its own. You should live a life that marries the spiritual and the physical and not favor one over the other.

You must deal with other problems when this chakra is out of balance because you feel much fear when you see visions, which drains you physically, emotionally, and mentally. You also deal with insomnia, nausea, seizures, sinus issues, vision issues, and terrible headaches. Later on in this chapter, you will learn what to do to open your third eye and keep it in balance.

The Pineal Gland

This gland is what connects the physical to the spiritual. It can help you ignite the supernatural abilities within you and use them for whatever you desire. It is the seat of ethereal energy, which you need to flesh out your psychic talents fully. The pineal gland also works with your hypothalamus, another gland that handles thirst, hunger, sexual desire, and your biological clock. It's the third eye and works in conjunction with the pituitary gland.

Your Ajna is the reason you get inspired, express creativity, gain wisdom and insight that others do not, connect with otherworldly beings, and have a sense of vision. With this chakra, you can get in touch with your intuition, exercise your psychic abilities of clairvoyance, clairaudience, and even more. You use it to see auras and other energy forms all around you.

When you awaken this chakra, you will have a rich inner world of perception. You will see visions, which depend on your way of receiving them. Sometimes the visions are blurry; other times, they are crisp and clear.

Blood flows more to your pineal gland than any other organ in your body, and it is also enveloped by cerebrospinal fluid. It has lots of melatonin in high concentrations. This melatonin is an antioxidant that combats stress and aging. It's also the reason you have a good night's sleep. It oversees your mood, immunity, and circadian rhythms. It's a photosensitive gland, which means light and darkness affect it, particularly regarding melatonin production. Light keeps it from creating melatonin, while darkness encourages it.

When the gland floods your system with melatonin, it moves around your brain and then heads to your blood vessels to reach all parts of your body. If you do not get adequate melatonin, you get mood swings, depression, and other disorders based on seasons. Melatonin is also responsible for helping you break down chemicals in your brain like pinoline and DMT, both of which handle physical and emotional processes.

Awakening Your Ajna

People think that once you wake this chakra up, that is it. However, you have to learn to keep it open, which means you must be at home with controlled relaxation and a soft yet focused awareness, which is the only way you can see beyond the illusions of the physical world and gain true knowledge and insight about what's going on.

Psychic Abilities

Psychic abilities are outside the realm of the world of action. They are activities that only happen in a paranormal or supernatural space, so, unfortunately, science, for the most part, discredits them. Again, science is so staunchly against the psychic reality because scientists—hilariously—try to measure the nonphysical using instruments created specifically to measure just physical phenomena based on observation with the physical senses. That is a topic for another day, but for now, here is a list of psychic abilities you could have right now and be unaware of:

Astral Projection: The ability to explore all other realms of consciousness and the physical by projecting your awareness from the physical plane to the astral plane through the separation of the astral body from your physical one.

Aura Reading: This is being able to perceive someone's aura or yours. It is the ability to read the energy of a person or thing and know immediately what is bothering them or what they're about now.

Automatic Writing: A form of writing without any sort of thought, on a conscious level. It's a form of channeling, in which you serve as a medium for some other being to pass along their message.

Bilocation: The ability to be in two (or more) places at the same time.

Channeling: This process involves allowing a spirit (or some other entity) to pass along its message through you by staying open. Popular channelers include the late Jane Roberts (who channeled Seth), Darryl Anka (who channels Bashar), Roxanne (who channels Bashar, Abraham, The Collective, and a host of others), and Esther Hicks, who channels Abraham (Abraham-Hicks to be precise since other channelers claim to speak for Abraham).

Clairalience: The ability to smell things that others cannot because the smell isn't physical in origin.

Clairaudience: The ability to hear things outside of human perception.

Claircognizance: The ability to know things that others don't pick up on. It's an instant, inexplicable knowing, often with no logical reason for why you should know that information at all. It's not information you arrive at through deductive reasoning or guesswork.

Clairgustance: The ability to taste things that are outside the human perception.

Clairsentience: The ability to sense things that others can't. For instance, you might be able to sense the presence of a being that others don't notice.

Clairvoyance: The ability to see things that exist outside of normal human perception. Not to be confused with hallucinations.

Divination: The ability to gain insight and knowledge about circumstances using rituals or other tools.

Dowsing: With this ability, you can find an object no matter where it is.

Healing: You can fix health situations by using energy. You can also heal the emotional and mental wounds this way.

Levitation: The ability to float or fly.

Precognition: The ability to tell what's going to happen in the future. It's not based on logical deductive reasoning but is akin to an inexplicable knowing and may be accompanied by dreams and visions.

Psychokinesis: The ability to move objects around using mental energy.

Psychometry: The ability to glean information about someone, something, an event, or a memory, just by touching an object connected to any of them.

Retrocognition: The ability to perceive events that happened in the past when you weren't even there. Again, this is not based on deductive reasoning or guesswork.

Scrying: Using a tool to see into the future or see the way ahead of yourself in terms of distance.

Telepathy: The ability to communicate words, thoughts, and feelings from your mind to another's mind, as well as being able to read what other people are thinking.

So how do you discover what abilities you have? How do you begin to develop them? By opening your third eye. Now, it is time to get into that!

Opening Your Third Eye

1. *Learn to silence your mind.* You can do this through meditation, spending more time in nature, or creating art. You need a calm mind to read the information coming from the other side.

2. *Work on your intuition.* This means you need to practice trusting your gut more and more so that you can begin to get even clearer messages from it. You could look into horoscopes and tarot cards to get started.

3. *Allow yourself to be creative.* As you get creative, your rational mind loosens up, letting go of its firm grasp on the part of you that knows more than it could ever hope to know. Indulge in imagination and allow it to lead you. This stimulates your third eye.

4. *Remain grounded always.* If you aren't, you might find the messages you receive to be very troubling. Visualize the earth's energy coming up from the ground, flowing into your body through your feet, and rooting your instability.

Now, you will get into the pineal gland and what it has to do with waking your third eye up. While the pituitary gland is the master gland—in that it controls all the other glands and the hormones they create in your body—the pineal gland is level with your eyes and smack dab in the middle of your brain, above and behind the pituitary gland. It's responsible for all extrasensory perception and your mystical experiences and psychic powers. Here is what you need to do to boost its function:

1. *Meditate.* The more you meditate, the more this gland is stimulated, and your nervous system is kept balanced.

2. *Go out in the sun and bask in it as often as you can.* Sunlight is a great way to wake up the gland. You can try sungazing, including at dawn and dusk. In the bright afternoon sun, you can shut your eyes and lift your face to the sky, focusing on your brow chakra.

3. *Spend time in the dark.* This means all lights off. When you do this, your pineal gland secretes healthy doses of its hormones and remains healthy and active.

4. *Eat clean, good food.* Do away with junk food, and make sure you don't eat heavy dinners. Cap your eating at six pm at the latest.

5. *Practice tapping.* Tap your brow chakra on your forehead. As you tap, the vibrations wake up your pineal gland and get your pituitary gland and hypothalamus going too.

6. *Breathe properly to encourage a stronger flow of cerebrospinal fluid.*

7. *Squeeze your eyes shut to activate the pituitary gland.* Suck in your cheeks to get the cranial pumps going as well.

8. *Chant often to get your cerebrospinal fluid and melatonin going.*

9. *Laugh and smile as often as you can.* This opens your crown and heart chakras, allowing more divine light to flow through you, boosting chi and blood flow, which also activates your pineal gland.

10. *Press your tongue against the roof of your mouth.*

11. *You can also wake up the gland by simply being aware of your third eye chakra and keeping your awareness on it for ten to fifteen minutes each time.*

12. *Wear colors that represent your third eye chakra.* You can also make sure your space is full of colors within the same hue.

13. *Eat foods that are naturally blue and purple.* You may juice them if you prefer.

14. *Start keeping a dream journal.* The more you write down your dreams, the more you remember, and the more your third eye opens.

15. *Make use of essential oils to cleanse your chakra.* Grapefruit, nutmeg, myrrh, German or Roman chamomile, and Sandalwood work wonders.

Your Ajna Stones

Use gemstones, healing stones, and crystals to open and balance your chakra. Every stone has unique characteristics, energy, and uses. Here are some stones you should consider using for your third eye:

- *Purple Fluorite:* This is a semi-precious stone that gives you clarity of thought and improves your focus. It helps you get more in touch with your intuition and actively banishes all negativity. You can use it to bring balance to your Ajna or stimulate it.

- *Black Obsidian:* This helps you remove all blocks in your chakras and dispels all negative energy. It will give you more control over your emotion. It brings balance to you and stimulates your Ajna.

- *Moldavite:* This dark-green stone is great for boosting your dream recall and giving the clarity of your dreams. It can balance your entire chakra system, clear out negativity, bring balance, stimulate your chakras, and keep them clean.

- *Amethyst:* This comes in shades from dark to light purple. It's a stone that brings healing, keeps you safe from all harm, and brings you wisdom. It will restore balance to you, stimulate your third eye, and open it.

Do all that you can to stimulate your third eye, and with time, you will begin to unlock your psychic abilities. Continue to work with these abilities as they get stronger with constant practice.

Chapter Eight: Mystical Manifestation — The (Real) Law of Attraction

You cannot learn the subject of mysticism without talking about the Law of Attraction. In a nutshell, this law states that things of similar energies attract each other. It is basically "opposites attract" flipped on its head. You have probably given thought to the origins of this law and how it may or may not have changed over the centuries. Do people now have a better grasp of this law in terms of using it to manifest our desired realities?

The fact of the matter is that there is no better way to learn about the law than to put it into practice yourself. This is covered in this chapter, but first, you need to delve into the law of attraction's origins and where the idea of manifesting your desires comes from. You will look at the actual science behind this law and how its meaning has morphed over the years.

The History of the Law of Attraction

The law has its roots in Eastern mysticism. Back then, it wasn't referred to as the "Law of Attraction." You could find it in Christian as well as Buddhist teachings. According to the Buddha, people are the sum of their thoughts. According to Jesus, we all can create amazing, wondrous things for ourselves.

Most people believe that in some way, people have always known of this law since it has always affected them since they were babies. The only reason they became conscious of this law was thanks to Madame Helena Petrovna Blavatsky.

During the nineteenth century, the New Thought movement was born, and this is what ushered the concept of manifestation into stardom. Certain authors were very instrumental in the growth and development of this idea, and you would be remiss not to acknowledge all the work that Madame Helena Blavatsky and Thomas Troward did in making the idea even clearer today.

Blavatsky toured various countries during the nineteenth century, giving her guidance on the law of attraction and other spiritual matters. Everyone knew that she had spiritual talents. She worked with her knowledge about old religious practices to write the original secret, titled *The Secret Doctrine*. Everything she penned down is now part of what is known as the "Law of Attraction" today. In her view, the way people think about who they are and how they identify themselves are responsible for the life they live and the things they've achieved so far. For her, everyone can change their reality and break free of limitations.

She proposed that the world around you is first created within you, and in that light, there is no reason to be afraid of the things that trouble you because all problems are opportunities for greatness in disguise. You only need to be willing to develop yourself to experience the safety and success that you desire.

Thomas Troward also did a fair bit of work in the nineteenth century that affects how people see the law of attraction today. Back in his time, he was called the "mystic Christian." Along with Madame Blavatsky, he was a proponent of growing spiritually by looking to the teachings of a diverse range of religions and traditions.

Troward viewed the mind as being divine in its function. For him, the only reason anyone is ever limited is that they believe they are limited. By implication, a belief in your unlimited nature would lead to much better results in whatever you set your mind to do. He also believed that your thoughts and actions must be congruent. In other words, it's not enough to simply think of one thing and then do something contrary. You must act in a way that aligns with what you profess or claim to believe.

By the start of the twentieth century, word on the law of attraction began to spread rapidly. Many authors began to put out their ideas on the Law and how to use it to manifest. Some of them were, of course, more prominent than others. However, they all contributed to the understanding of the idea today and were responsible for a lot of the terminologies used.

For William Walker Atkinson, it was important for the law practitioner to focus on improving their focus, willpower, and magnetism to allow more good into their lives. This man wrote over a hundred books in his lifetime, and all while practicing law. He wanted nothing more than to teach people how to use the law of attraction and always asked for readers to develop his ideas even further. He was heavily inspired by some Hindi teachings and even worked a lot with Hindus. Even now, people use some ideas that he gave in his teachings, such as the concept of vibration.

Also of prominence is Wallace D. Wattles, who wrote the classic *The Science of Getting Rich*, published in 1910. Even today, people continue to read his work, in which he made it clear that people have to focus on growing and developing their potential for manifestation instead of waiting for experts on the subject to spoon-feed them.

Napoleon Hill gave the treasure that is *Think and Grow Rich* in 1937. The difference between Hill and the others is that he had no religious influences. He is why you now know that when you allow yourself to have negative thoughts, you will only create reasons for you to continue thinking that way. He was a big proponent of discovering your passion and following it.

By the eighties, Esther and Jerry Hicks gave the Teachings of Abraham, which took the law of attraction and made the concept incredibly simple to use for everyone. They made the process easy and clear and have even provided exercises you can do to create the life you desire after Abraham came to Rhonda Byrne with her book (and film) titled *The Secret,* which put the law of attraction on the map. They were a huge success and spread the word to one and all about how the law of attraction can indeed work if you use it right.

The Tools for the Law of Attraction

You want to know how to make use of this law, so now you will learn about the tools you can use to make your desires come through.

Tool #1: Sexual Transmutation — You can't deny that there's something powerful about sexual desire. During the act, you are single-minded. It's almost like meditation. Seen through to its end, it can lead to the creation of life itself. In other words, your sexual energy creates life, and you can use this same energy to manifest the big stuff you desire.

Your sexual drive is governed by the sacral chakra, which is also called the sex center, where all sexual energy is stored. In Qigong, it is known as the Dantien. When you have sex, the energy comes out and forms a human life. Yes, this has been mentioned already, but this is worth repeating. Stop and think about the sort of power required to form another human being. Wouldn't you say it's pretty much a miracle? It should make you wonder if there are other things you can create with your sexual energy.

When you transmute that energy toward your desires, they have no chance but to come to pass. Napoleon Hill discovered something about the successful people in life: They tend to have an insatiably high sex drive. Sure, there are those with a lot of lust and a lot of nothing in their bank accounts. That's most likely because they aren't channeling their sexual energy toward their manifestation. Successful people know how to use the energy to create their desires.

You can move that energy upward through your sacral chakra and up to your pineal gland or third eye chakra, opening that chakra better and faster than other techniques for opening the third eye. The sexual energy is very high and very intense, which makes it perfect for manifesting using the law of attraction. You will notice that athletes have periods when they don't have sex. There are many anecdotes about how athletes having sex decreases their performance in their sport. You simply must use the energy the right way.

Here is how it works:

1. Lock your root chakra by squeezing your pelvic muscles, just like you would if you were trying not to have an accident before getting to the bathroom. So, lock your root, and then inhale.

2. As you inhale, the energy cannot escape from your root chakra and has nowhere to go but up to the sacral chakra.

3. As you exhale, tighten your sacral chakra area in a lock.

4. Inhale again, moving the energy to your solar plexus chakra. Exhale into a lock, squeezing in that area.

5. Move that energy up through the heart chakra, and the throat chakra, up to your pineal gland. This will activate your pineal gland, and your third eye will open. You will know it's open because you'll start to see colors.

6. At this point, you want to visualize or imagine yourself having achieved your desires and dreams.

This is the fastest way to manifest your desires; the energy you moved from below to above will now be directed toward whatever you have visualized.

Tool #2: Gratitude — Simply making a practice of showing gratitude for the good things in your life will cause even more goodness to come your way. All you need to do is get a journal and take some time to write down a list of all you appreciate in life at the start and end of your day. Just three to five items will do each time.

Tool #3: Focus Wheels — Here is how to use these:

1. Draw a very big circle on a piece of paper. Make sure it's a big enough circle that touches the edges of the paper.

2. Then draw another smaller circle within it, in the center.

3. Divide the space between both circles into twelve parts and keep the inner circle empty.

4. Set your intention, which is whatever you want to accomplish by using this focus wheel.

5. In these twelve spaces, you're going to write a sentence each that starts with the phrase "I love." Each sentence should be about the parts of your life you love the most.

6. Write this with the energy of love and gratitude in your heart, truly pondering what you love and are thankful for. Your intention could be for a more supportive family or more wealth coming in.

7. If you can't find anything that you're truly thankful for, you can simply write down any sentences that reflect the idea of what you want. For instance, if your intention is abundance, but you don't have an abundance of anything in your life, you could write about the abundance of air, leaves on a tree, raindrops, etc.

8. After filling all twelve segments, write your highest, most significant intention in the inner circle. Make sure you frame it positively and in the present tense.

Tool #3: Visualization — All you must do is shut your eyes and imagine yourself accomplishing whatever it is you set out to do. Say you want to manifest love, you can imagine holding hands, being kissed, falling asleep at night while being held, a wedding ring on your finger, or whatever else would imply you have your desire.

Tool #4: Meditation — As you meditate, you will train yourself to be more in vibrational alignment with all good things, including your desire. Make it a daily practice, and you'll start to notice how quickly your manifestations come to you.

Tool #5: Affirmations — With this tool, just state your intentions over and over, phrasing it positively and in the present tense. Don't say, "Love is coming to me." Say, "I am in love." Don't say, "I don't want to be poor" over and over. Instead, say, "I am wealthy."

Tool #6: Brainwave Entrainment — You can download brainwave entrainment mp3s, like binaural beats or isochronic tones. Scientifically, they help you with your manifesting by bringing balance to both hemispheres of your brain, helping you to focus and receive what you imagine or visualize.

Tool #7: Vision Boards — You're going to need a board for this one or some cardboard you can stick to a wall. Cut out or print out pictures that represent your desires. Go ahead and write down words that also inspire you. Put that board up where you'll see it first thing in the morning and last thing at night.

Tool #8: Act "As If" — This is probably one of the easiest ways to get your desire. You want to act as if it's already a done deal. This doesn't mean you go around telling people you are rich, or have a lover, or are healed when they can clearly see you aren't. It means you should do those things that you would have to do if you were rich, in love, healthy, or had whatever you wanted. Being rich means you have no choice but to learn about where to park your money, so it yields more, and how to make your money work for you, as well as how to save on taxes. Being in love means you must decide what kind of life you have together and make room in your life for the other person. As a healthy person, you would take walks, which could turn into runs. You'd choose celery over cookies. This is how to act as if.

Tool #9: Make a List of Positives — It's almost like the gratitude list, except that in this case, you can go ahead and mention not just the stuff that's working out already, but everything that you're looking forward to. What this does is put you in a frame of mind of positive expectation. When you expect something good to happen to you, good must come! So, go ahead and write down all the things you're looking forward to being, doing, having, and experiencing in your life.

Tool #10: Set Goals — The real reason that goal setting works, even for those who don't believe in the law of attraction, is because it is the law of attraction at work! When you set a goal, you focus your intention and attention on experiencing a certain manifestation, whether it's with fitness, your career, wealth, or whatever you want to make better. So, try setting goals and see how well that works. You should write it down somewhere conspicuous, where you'll see it every day. When you write it down, it brings even more focus and makes it more concrete for you. Also, you should set a time frame for that goal. For instance, you could write, "By this time next year, I will have made my first million dollars."

Tool #11: Record and Listen to Yourself — There are apps out there like Think Up that allows you to record affirmations that you can listen to either as you meditate, work, or in the form of subliminal while you play your favorite tunes. When you listen to this message repeatedly, you will find your life shifting to reflect the message's truth. This is a very powerful one. Try listening to it every night when you're sleepy as well, and you will get potent results.

Tool #12: Emotional Freedom Techniques — This is also called EFT, or more commonly, tapping. Use tapping to get rid of any blocks in your energy and any limiting beliefs you may hold on to. All you have to do is tap on your body's acupuncture points while you express genuine positive emotions using your words. There is much to cover on acupressure points, but this topic is beyond this book's scope. That said, it is well worth looking into.

Tool #13: Be a Beacon of Positivity — Every day, in every way, make a point to do good, share good, and feel good. Make a point of making someone else feel good about themselves today. Give compliments that you mean and help someone out who could never pay you back. Choose to forgive and let go, rather than criticize or get angry. Choose to find the good in everything instead of complaining. When you're very active in being positive in deed, thought, and feeling, when you make it your duty to help others see even just a little bit that it is good in life, not by talking their ears off about it but by being an example of this idea, you will start to receive more and more good things in turn. That's just the way this works.

Chapter Nine: Astral Projection or OBEs

Astral projection is also called out of body experience or OBE because that is exactly what it is. It's when you deliberately leave your physical body and move your consciousness to the astral plane. You do not just have a physical body; you have an astral one, and other ones like the mental and causal bodies—but those are outside the scope of this chapter.

Astral projection is a practice as old as humans, and you will find records of it across many cultures. It is thanks to Theosophy that the term "astral projection" exists to begin with. It is closely connected with dreams, except it's much more stable and intense. The good news is that you do not have to be a shaman to project your consciousness to the astral plane. You can achieve this through meditation and very specific methods.

Hermeticism, Theosophy, Neoplatonism, and Rosicrucianism all see the astral light as a body that connects your mental body to the physical one, and the astral body as one that resides in a light world between Earth and Heaven. According to these schools of thought, this world has demons, angels, and all sorts of spirits and astral beings.

Your astral body is connected to your physical one through a silver cord, according to some thoughts. Others feel that this is only a metaphor. Depending on which version you buy into, you may or may not see a silver cord during your astral travels. If you are a Christian and wondering if you should even try to project, it may interest you to know that Paul wrote in 2 Corinthians about "a man in Christ who fourteen years ago was caught up to the third heaven. Whether it was in the body or out of the body, I do not know — God knows." He didn't seem to condemn it, so you should be golden.

Astral Projection Across Different Cultures

In ancient Egypt, there was much to be said about the soul or ba, which floats just outside your regular body, which the Egyptians call ka. In Chinese Taoism, there is Qingfu, who fell asleep, and when he did, his "primordial spirit" went off to a banquet room to address some people, who had found that while the actual Qingfu slept, there was also another right there with them, in the same clothes, with the same face.

In Hinduism, you have concepts like the Linga Sarira, which you can find in Valmiki's Yog Vashishta-Maha Ramayan. There is also the case of a miracle carried out by Swami Pranabananda in astral form, as witnessed by Paramahansa Yogananda. According to Meher Baba, a self-proclaimed avatar, there needs to be some preparation for the process of projection. You need to demonstrate that you can be trusted to use your astral body responsibly, and after that, you can journey in your astral body by leaving your physical one while asleep or even while awake. He taught that it matters a lot that you are fully conscious when you project, which means spontaneous projections that happen on their own do not count. You must consciously use your body, as this helps you learn just how true it is that you are not mere flesh. Think of your body as a coat you can take off and put on whenever you like—except that each time you take it off and put it back on, you become more spiritually advanced.

Japanese mythology talks about ikisudama, which is your soul away from your body. There is also the belief that if someone does something wrong to you, or you do not like them, or deeply cannot stand them for some reason, your ikisudama can leave your body (in part or wholly), appear before this person you don't like, and harm or curse them in some way. This is why people wear bracelets and amulets to ward off the "evil eye," which is a hateful glare people send your way when you're not aware. They also believe that your soul will leave your body when you're in a coma or sick.

Inuit people have those who can travel to places without moving their physical body, and they come back to share what they saw and did with the rest of the community. They return with valuable information about how to heal the sick, get better at hunting, find more prey, and so on.

The Wai-Wai of Northern Brazil and Guyana have the yaskomo, who can go on a "soul flight" for various purposes like consulting with the divine, healing, getting names for newborns, and so forth.

What's in the Astral World?

First, the astral world is made up of different levels. The one you land in depends on your state of consciousness. Each level has its beings and forms that reside within it. The astral world is made up of emotions and thoughts, creating various astral forms or attracting them. One thing you will notice in the astral is that your thoughts do become things. Having an astral projection truly is a crash course in the law of attraction in that regard.

The astral world is not a place you can categorize based on physical metrics like temperature, economic prosperity, productivity, or anything of the sort. It is all about consciousness and its varying levels. There are three basic levels you should bother with:

- The lower astral planes
- The desire planes

• Summerland

Lower Astral: This area doesn't have much light. Souls that are deep in the doldrums of despair and helplessness are often trapped here. You might see some very ugly creatures here, and they may not make any sense to you at all if they try to communicate with you. It is like being in a nightmare, except it's a lot more intense because, as any experienced astral projector will tell you, the astral world feels even more real than the physical one—which is admittedly tough for the inexperienced to fathom.

If you find yourself on this plane, do not despair. If you can find it within you to calm down, you will notice that amid the darkness, ugliness, and downright fearfulness, there's a guide or being nearby. You might not be able to see them, but just remembering this can help you sense that they're there and you're safe. You will learn that despite the ugliness of this place, you should show love to all the beings there, as it is only through love that they can be set free.

Be warned that you might never want to go to the astral project again if you find yourself in this plane. So, don't let that deter you. There is so much more to explore. You will not die there, and you could never get lost there. Those beings you see are simply lost souls and nothing more. Show them love to set them free, and in doing so, you will lift your consciousness up and out of that level to higher ones.

The Desire Planes: Desire is very important in that it dictates where your project to. Desire is a good thing that only goes bad when you allow yourself to become enslaved by it. This is a level that mirrors day-to-day living. You will notice that your surroundings are the same as if you were awake within your physical body. However, there is a catch: You can walk through walls, drop through the floor, or fly on out through the roof because there's no solid matter to serve as an obstacle.

You can move through these things as though they're just air. You can see the people around you doing their own thing as you move about, and no, they will not be able to see you or respond to you—unless they're particularly sensitive to auras and energies. However, children can see astral projectors going about their business because they don't have any restrictions on their minds yet about what is possible. If you've got a dog, don't be surprised if they can see you too.

The Summerland: This is a term that Theosophists, Spiritualists, and Wiccans have adopted to describe a place of rest that lies between one lifetime and the next. There is no obstacle to deal with and no judgment to confront. It is just like Heaven; it's the highest level of the astral, where you can unite with your loved ones that have passed on before you. This is the level where you will find many teachers, guides, and angels who work to help you find your feet in that plane.

If you wind up in Summerland, the desire to just remain is intense. Coming back to the physical can leave you with a feeling of nostalgia, loss, or an aching longing to go back "home" because it feels like what the phrase "coming home" is supposed to be.

In the astral plane, you will find helpers whose job is to help those struggling because they're stuck in the lower planes or have a purpose that they need to fulfill on Earth. They don't stick around for long like guides do; they will only help for the short term, complete their mission, and then move on.

Some guides teach you to become more than who you are. You cannot mistake the vibration of love that flows from them and the sense that they know you even more than you know yourself. They come from the higher realm, the mental and causal planes, and put on an astral body so that they can relate with those on that plane. If they don't, their radiance will be way too much for those in the astral to bear. They help those on that plane get ready to move on to the next level, the mental plane.

You'll also find occupants that aren't human. They include various thought-forms, which are drawn to those who are a match to them. You can also find animals on the astral plane—although they don't stick around for too long. Finally, you will also find some debris, which are thought-forms that are no longer useful and are dying out. Think of them as shells of those souls that have gone on to the mental plane. Sometimes, a thought-form can take on the shell for its purposes, but that shell is no longer viable after a while, as it breaks down and is recycled.

Signs You're About to Astral Project

Here are some things you will experience when you are about to leave your body. These are not all required signs, but you will have some of them:

- Vibrations all over your body
- A roaring sound or buzzing in your head
- The sound of voices nearby, either talking, singing
- Feeling your heartbeat fast
- Feeling your eyes turning up
- Hearing popping sounds
- Hearing explosions

It is not unusual to first hear something, whether it's a hum, buzz, roaring, or ringing sound. It continues on and on and is very hypnotic. These all create some pressure in your head but do not let this frighten you. For you to successfully project, you must relax.

You might also feel some irritation on your skin or a prickly sensation. This is also normal. After this, you will notice your muscles are paralyzed. This is catalepsis, where your body is still to keep you from sleepwalking or acting out your dream.

When you get to this point, the sound will reach unbearable levels. Your heart beats fast, and your breathing changes. Then you get the idea that there are two of you, which happens when your astral body is leaving the physical.

How to Prepare for Astral Projection

You need to be safe when you travel. You might be tempted to overlook this, but don't. You would not travel to another country without your passport and papers, vaccines, and insurance, would you? It is the same with astral travel. The astral plane, like real life, is made up of beings both benevolent and malevolent. You want to be safe since you are a new visitor. Rest assured that your guides are with you, but don't rely on them to handle everything for you.

Do not take any substances that would lead to you feeling high or drunk—no, hallucinogens. Also, do not watch anything that will engage you emotionally or mentally before bed, especially stuff with horror or violence. If you do, don't be surprised when you attract the kinds of beings you would rather cross to the other side of the astral road to avoid. Ensure that you're emotionally happy and at peace, as this will greatly enhance the quality of your experience. Thoughts are things, so whatever you do, check all negative thoughts and emotions at the door.

Finally, you have no business trying to astral project if you are not stable emotionally and mentally or have mental health issues. It is not that you would be in any danger; it's just that you shouldn't try to project unless you have someone you can turn to who knows the difference between a projection and psychosis. It is a sad situation that, for the most part, many scientists and doctors think astral projection is psychosis in action.

How to Astral Project

Keep in mind that this is a skill, and like all skills, practice makes perfect. Patience will also be required. If you want to learn more about astral projection, you should look up Robert Munroe's explorations outside the body. Here are some rules to follow before you begin:

1. You must not be disturbed. Switch off your phone, and make sure there are no alarms. Let your family know you do not want to be disturbed. Keep pets away, as they'll want to be close to you when you're engaged in any psychic activity.

2. Get as comfy as you can in bed.

3. Make sure your clothing is very comfortable and loose.

4. Make sure the temperature is just right. You don't want to feel too hot or too cold, or you'll feel suffocated or find it hard to focus.

5. Lie down in a way that allows you to project easily. This means on your back, arms by your side. You might wake up with your arms crossed on your chest. This is a normal position that is meant to protect you.

6. Get control of your breathing. Make sure your breaths are nice, long, and easy. Take your time exhaling. Make sure you're not using any effort or strain and that you relax your body with each breath, moving from your toes up to your head, relaxing the muscles in your face, keeping your throat relaxed, and your jaw. You will find it best to allow your mouth to be slightly open.

It is okay to have to practice all these several times before finally getting the hang of utter relaxation while remaining conscious. After some time, you will notice a buzz or hum in your head, which grows stronger or weaker depending on your consciousness. Just make peace with all the sounds and everything else going on. Let the sensations take over you, and continue to relax further and further, making sure not to get excited, as this can snap you right out of it. Your first ride will be a bit rough, but that's okay. It's the difference between the first time you got on a plane and the most recent time you got on one.

After a bit, the humming or buzzing will even out. The roar dies down to more of a purr, like that of a motorbike. If you notice that the sound is fading, bring it back because if you do not, you will wind up falling asleep, and you won't remember a thing.

Once the buzzing has evened out, it is time to get out of your body. Don't make this hard work, because it isn't. It will happen. If you get excited, calm down. If you get fearful, relax and remember that you are safe, and there is always a guide with you. Don't worry about smacking your head against the ceiling or wall, or you'll snap back into your body. Just trust that you are fine.

On your first trip, you probably won't be able to control where you go or whom you meet. Do not let this bother you. The more you practice, the better you will get. The more you visit the astral plane, the better you will be at going there and moving around. You will note that you can fly, teleport, see things in 360 degrees, and so much more.

When you come back from your travels, you must write down everything you experienced. It is a good way to make sure you do not forget and reinforces the idea in your subconscious mind that astral projection matters and that remembering your projections matter, so you are more than likely to succeed at both.

Chapter Ten: Habits of the Modern Mystic

Being a mystic in today's world is a very brave thing to do, especially as most people are quick to dismiss the reality of things beyond the physical. If you have chosen this route, you deserve to be applauded for doing your bit to raise the world's consciousness. Everyone has all the technology and scientific advancements, but most people are underdeveloped, poor, and wretched when it comes to mystical matters. Choosing the mystic path means that you are giving back to the world, ushering in an era of spiritual enlightenment.

Now, here is the thing about being a mystic: You do not get a day off. It is your life now. You should be willing to make certain practices a habit because this is the only way to continue growing in psychic development and maintaining your connection with the spiritual. This isn't a fad, and you cannot check out of it like you would a video game. So, the first thing you need to do is think about where your interest lies in mystical matters, and then you should begin to pursue that.

Habits of the Modern-Day Mystic

- *Think like a mystic.* The thing about mystics is that in all the chaos, they can find order and meaning. So, you must do the same thing by looking for evidence of the divine at work, no matter what's going on. As a mystic, you will begin to note every coincidence, for there is no such thing as coincidences. Notice the divine in all things. Know that there is a power within you that you can connect with to change your world for the better. Whichever mystical system of belief you have chosen, explore it, and dive deeper so you can have the correct mystical mindset.

- *Find the connection of all things in your life.* The mystic knows that all things are related, that nothing exists in a bubble. Your job is always to find the thread that binds all things together. You do not seek out how people or things are different, even if you don't particularly like those people or things; you see the common denominator that binds everyone. This also means that you shouldn't limit yourself to teachings that are in your mystical school of thought, but look to other disciplines as well, for you will find nuggets of truth that connect it all and tell the same story. Seek to be a uniting force, not a divisive one.

- *Make experience matter above all else.* Not a theory. You shouldn't just be a mystic in name, but a mystic in practice. It is not enough to read about stuff. Put it all to practice so that you will have experience on your side. It's nice to hear or read about other people's mystical experiences, but it is so much better to have your own because then you know that you're on a true path, and your faith grows. When your faith grows, that will inevitably lead to even more manifestations and even stronger and better psychic activity on your end. Be very wary of those who focus more on materialistic things. You don't have to have expensive koi ponds or mandalas to be a true mystic.

• *Be here, now.* As a mystic, you must be grounded and present always. You shouldn't be easily distracted by your phone, stress at work, or your very hectic daily schedule. Whatever you are doing now, focus on that and that alone. If you intend to sleep, set your phone down, and sleep. If it is to write, then write, and don't get distracted. If you're eating, just eat, and don't watch a show or read something while you're at it. Throw yourself completely into whatever you're doing now.

Unsurprisingly, this is very difficult to achieve at first. It's the world people live in today, with all the news, ads, devices, and social media deliberately crafted in such a way to get you addicted to every little ding. However, you can do this. All you need to do is start bit by bit. Practice not reaching for your phone first thing in the morning. Practice going out without it. Practice only giving yourself access to it when you need to make an important call or send an important message.

• *Always ask questions.* Don't just swallow everything you hear and read hook, line, and sinker. You want to question the information you get and test it out for yourself to see if it's true or if it works. If you want to become more and more in touch with the mystical, get comfortable asking uncomfortable questions. What is the point of your existence? Why are you on this little blue dot? Who are you—the real you? What will happen when you die? What do you think about death?

• *Trust your gut.* The more you do, the better you'll get at reading it, and it will never steer you wrong. Trusting your gut will always lead you to find the answers that you desire. Learn to trust your intuition and follow those inner nudges you get. Decide today that you're done doubting yourself and that you will always find the truth and pleasant places when you follow that little voice.

How to Build a Strong Foundation

You cannot just claim to be a mystic and then stop there. You need a springboard to launch your practice. So, take time out to read mystical books and ancient texts. This is the best way to learn what it is like to live like a true mystic and grow like one. The more you read, the more you will notice a connection between all the teachings, and they will blend seamlessly together. Here are some interesting books to begin with:

- *The Confessions of St. Augustine* by Saint Augustine
- The Nasruddin Stories from the Sufi
- *An Introduction To Zen Buddhism* by DT Suzuki
- *No Man Is An Island* by Thomas Merton
- *The Cloud of Unknowing* (author anonymous)
- *Revelations of Divine Love* by Julian of Norwich

Next, you must know what the central ideas of your mystical practice are. You must know the guidelines that regulate your practice and why you should do things the way you do them. Depending on which religion or viewpoint you align yourself with, your rituals, chants, and other things of that nature will be different. Learn the guidelines to discover what resonates with you and what matters the most to you.

For instance, there are Christians who are more about living just like Jesus lived, according to the Bible's account of the Holy Savior. There are other Christians who are more about going around and telling people about Jesus Christ. These are different ways that people choose to practice Christianity, and both principles are equally important. So, learn the principles of your faith, and discover what rings true for you so you can practice more of that and get great results.

Your spiritual practice should come first before anything else. Again, you do not get any days off from being a mystic. You need to make your practice the most important thing before your career, money, job, hobbies, or anything else. This is a tall order, but you must do your best to see it done each day. This is the reason most mystics are all on their own. It is not the easiest thing to do, being a mystic and going clubbing on Friday—not that there is anything wrong with clubbing; it's just that you might find it tough to juggle being regular and diving deep into the mystical. You must commit to this.

Finally, be at peace with the mystery of life. Certain things are beyond comprehension and just are the way they are. Do yourself a favor and learn to embrace that. In Zen meditation, you must embrace your void—which could be your bedroom or whatever space where you can just sit in quiet contemplation and acceptance of life being as it is. When you choose to trust your gut, sometimes, you will have more questions and no answers in sight. You could choose to feel frustrated by that, or you could feel the freedom in knowing that you do not know, you don't have all the answers to life's biggest mysteries, and that is perfectly okay.

The Mystical Way

Being a mystic means being spiritual—acknowledging and accepting the mysterious and that which is otherworldly. It means you know that science is great, and it is awesome, but that there are things science will never be able to explain fully but which are true anyway.

As a mystic, you are not unaware of the real world. You're not floating in a fantasy land; you're fully aware of life as it is, and you're not trying to claim it is not real. You understand that it is important to accept it all and that through this acceptance, you can take the right course of action.

That said, you are aware that the real world isn't only physical but spiritual. You know that there is an unseen realm, and you revel in it because there is power there that you can tap into to make the lives of those around you better and give your life meaning. You work with mystical energy and are guided by your intuition to choose the right course of action in the physical world.

You have a deep connection with the physical and nonphysical aspects of reality, and you know how to ground your mystical energy in practicality, for this is much more potent than simply playing in the spiritual realm alone. You know that your knowledge of life's deeper truths does not give you the license to misuse your knowledge. You are well aware that your higher insights do not exempt you from the law of karma, and with that in mind, you make a point of giving only light and love to one and all.

You understand the idea of Wu wei, which is the flow that exists in all of nature. Everything has its season and its time, and you know that there is no need for force when you simply trust the universe and allow it to do its part after you have done yours.

How to Dive Deeper into the Mystic Waters

If you want to succeed, make a point to meditate or pray and contemplate mystical truths every day. The more you meditate, the deeper your awareness of the mystical grows, and the better you will get at whatever mystical gift you have. When you meditate, you might not necessarily end every practice feeling like something happened. It is important to keep this in mind. Some days you feel amazing, and other days you feel nothing. Either way, the only thing that matters is discipline and consistency, which gives you results. Do not let one day of skipped meditations turn into three or a lifetime of no meditation. Make it a rule never to skip more than a day.

You must also be willing and ready to let go of all beliefs that do not serve you. This is why you need to study as much as you can, for the more you study, the lighter you have to look into your mind and see what it is that holds you back from even richer practices and experiences than you already have. There is a Zen saying that speaks of Zen as being a boat. When you have to go across a river, you use it. However, when you are on the other side, you do not take the boat with you because you no longer need it. So, if certain ideas or practices no longer serve you, do yourself a favor and just let them go right now. It is okay to be wrong. Be quick to accept that you didn't know any better. Be okay with the fact that you won't always be right and that there will always be so much more to learn. Many mystics started great, only to lose their light because they refused to accept that their way was not the best, and they refused to evolve past what they believed before. Don't let pride derail your mystical life. It just isn't worth it.

Conclusion

Congratulations on having read this far. This is a beginning, but there is so much more to experience along your journey. Here is the kicker, though: You must put what you learn into practice. If you want to experience the wonder of synchronicity, get to know your inner self, feel balance in your body, and demonstrate your psychic abilities, and then you must begin your practice right away.

There is a trap most people fall into when they read books on subject matters like this—they become head experts. They can tell you what the anahata is, they can tell you exactly how to lucid dream or leave your body, but they have no experience at all. Or they have that one experience, from that one time, and nothing more because they did not continue to develop themselves. This is not the path to greatness.

Truly, all of life would be much better if everyone were mystics—not just regular mystics, but true ones who have mastered the art of connecting to the divine energy of love and using it to eradicate suffering in whatever practice comes most naturally.

As you practice, get ready to experience a life filled with divinity and a restless desire to remain connected with the spiritual. This is a good thing—if you remember that the physical stuff (like taking care of your body, handling the bills, and so on) matter as well. You will experience moments of being alone and feeling like the odd one out and moments of intense bonding with others, especially those of like mind. Embrace it all. The solitude is as good as the company, always.

Your life is one that will have a unique blend of the blessed and the banal, the sacred and the profane. That is fine. Your job is to find a way to marry the two so that others can see your light and gravitate to it, and they, too, can find their connection to their Source, just like you have.

Do not end your study with this book. Take your time to seek out knowledge. Do not just stick to one school of thought either. Learn all you can—from Buddhists, Hindus, and Sufis, to Christians, Freemasons, Hyperians, and yes, even the Illuminati. About that last group, you will be shocked to find that much of what you know about the Illuminati is untrue and nothing more than lies and propaganda. You might shock yourself with the profound truths you learn.

In all your learning, remember to ask questions. When you get answers, do not just accept them. Put them to the test yourself. This is how you grow and learn what works and what doesn't. No one came here to parrot one another. Everyone has unique paths. They may start following the same main route, but in the end, they must all branch off to pursue the truth of life and spirit in their way. Develop the mystic's spirit of adventure and exploration.

Here's another book by Mari Silva that you might like

MARI SILVA

NORSE MAGIC
FOR BEGINNERS
The Ultimate Guide to Norse Divination, Reading Elder Futhark Runes, and Spells

Your Free Gift (only available for a limited time)

Thanks for getting this book! If you want to learn more about various spirituality topics, then join Mari Silva's community and get a free guided meditation MP3 for awakening your third eye. This guided meditation mp3 is designed to open and strengthen ones third eye so you can experience a higher state of consciousness. Simply visit the link below the image to get started.

https://spiritualityspot.com/meditation

References

BBC. "Spiritualism at a glance." September 22, 2009. https://www.bbc.co.uk/religion/religions/spiritualism/ataglance/glance.s html

Cameron, Yogi. "A Beginner's Guide To The 7 Chakras." Mindbodygreen. April 23, 2019. https://www.mindbodygreen.com/0-91/The-7-Chakras-for-Beginners.html

Dale, Cyndi, "Energetic Anatomy: A Complete Guide to the Human Energy Fields and Etheric Bodies." Conscious Lifestyle Magazine. October 11, 2016. https://www.consciouslifestylemag.com/human-energy-field-aura/

Encyclopedia Britannica. "Techniques for inducing mystical experiences." Accessed?. https://www.britannica.com/topic/mysticism/Techniques-for-inducing-mystical-experiences

E.O.C.T.O. "Ancient Greek Mysticism | Celestial Order and Temple of Olympus." Accessed?. http://www.eocto.org/article/103

Faragher Kelly, Aliza. "Am I Psychic? How to Tap Into Your Own Psychic Abilities." Allure.

July 2, 2018.

https://www.allure.com/story/am-i-psychic-how-to-tap-into-psychic-abilities

Hinduwebsite.com. "Esoteric Mystic Hinduism," Accessed? https://www.hinduwebsite.com/esoterichinduism.asp

Horvath, Timmie. "Being an Everyday Mystic in a Modern World (A Mystic's Manifesto)." The Sacred Wellness School of Healing Arts. July 27, 2018.

https://www.sacredwellness.co/being-an-everyday-mystic-in-a-modern-world-a-mystics-manifesto/

Hurst, Katherine. "Law Of Attraction History: The Origins Of The Law Of Attraction Uncovered." The Law Of Attraction. June 5, 2019.

https://www.thelawofattraction.com/history-law-attraction-uncovered/

Fandom. "Mystic Wikia," Accessed?. https://mystic.fandom.com

Frantzis, Bruce. "Taoist Breathing." Energy Arts. April 26, 2014.

https://www.energyarts.com/taoist-breathing/

Jessica. "Third Eye — 6 Easy Exercises to Open that Baby Up." Intuitive Souls Blog. November 7, 2016.

https://intuitivesoulsblog.com/third-eye/

Kahn, Nina, and Neal, Brandi. "What You Should Know About Literal Out-Of-Body Experiences." Bustle. October 9, 2020.

https://www.bustle.com/life/what-is-astral-projection-heres-what-to-know-about-literal-out-of-body-experiences-12253529

Kaivalya, Alanna. "Life in Balance 101: A Modern Mystic's Guide to Keeping Calm and Carrying On." Alanna Kaivalya, Ph.D. June 30, 2017.

https://alannak.com/spirituality/life-in-balance-101-a-modern-mystics-guide-to-keeping-calm-and-carrying-on/

Lee, Ilchi. "Did You Know You Can Sense Energy? Here's How." Change Your Energy. October 31, 2013.

https://www.changeyourenergy.com/blog/712/did-you-know-you-can-sense-energy-heres-how

Marc. "The Tao Te Ching." The Mystical Path. September 22, 2017. https://contemplatingtruth.wordpress.com/2017/09/22/the-tao-te-ching/

McKinnley, Trish. "What is an Energy Ball & How do I Create One?" October 30, 2019. https://www.trishmckinnley.com/how-to-create-an-energy-ball/

Mindbliss. "What is the Pineal Gland's Function and How to Amplify It." June 4, 2018. https://mindbliss.com/pineal-gland-function-and-activation/

Motherhood Community. "This Is How Buddhist Taught Breathing Meditation." May 8, 2020. https://www.calmwithyoga.com/buddhist-monks-taught-breathe/

Mystic Visualization. "Creative Visualization and the Law of Attraction." Accessed?. http://mysticvisualization.com/the-law-of-attraction-and-creative-visualization/

Petroff, Elizabeth Alvilda. "The Mystics." Christian History Institute. Accessed?. https://christianhistoryinstitute.org/magazine/article/women-in-medieval-church-mystics

Reportace's Blog. "Mysticism: The Buddhist Approach." December 31, 2011. https://acestrada.wordpress.com/2011/12/31/mysticism-the-buddhist-approach

Shape. "6 Reasons You *Think* You Hate Meditation—and How to Fix Them." Accessed?.

https://www.shape.com/lifestyle/mind-and-body/beginners-guide-meditation

Share, Taylor. "How To Start Meditating: The Ultimate Guide For Beginner's Meditation." Nerd

Fitness. December 31, 2019.

https://www.nerdfitness.com/blog/meditation-building-the-superpower-you-didnt-even-know-you-had/

Sol, Mateo. "How to Induce a Trance State For Deep Psychospiritual Work." LonerWolf. October 22, 2018. https://lonerwolf.com/trance-state/

The Sacred Science. "A Breathing Exercise To Take You Higher." March 2, 2016. https://www.thesacredscience.com/a-breathing-exercise-to-take-you-higher/

CPSIA information can be obtained
at www.ICGtesting.com
Printed in the USA
BVHW060547270321
603526BV00011B/2261